Sweet & Salty

RECIPES

pil

Publications International, Ltd.

Louis Weber, CEO
Publications International, Ltd.
8140 Lehigh Ave
Morton Grove, IL 60053

Permission is never granted for commercial purposes.

Photograph on front cover copyright © Shutterstock.com.

Pictured on the front cover: Dipped, Drizzled & Decorated Pretzels (*page 174*).

Pictured on the back cover (*clockwise from top right*): Sweet Potato Maki Bowl (*page 70*), Peanut Butter & Jelly Monkey Biscuits (*page 172*), Peanut Butter & Chocolate Swirls (*page 142*) and Strawberry Chicken Salad (*page 64*).

ISBN: 978-1-63938-605-5

Manufactured in China.

8 7 6 5 4 3 2 1

Let's get social!
 @Publications_International
@PublicationsInternational
www.pilbooks.com

Table of Contents

Breakfast

Toast & Sausage Skewers

Makes 6 servings

1 package (8 ounces) refrigerated crescent dough sheet

1 package (about 12 ounces) fully cooked breakfast sausage links

Maple syrup

1 Preheat broiler. Unroll crescent dough; cut dough into thin strips (one for each sausage). Skewer sausages onto bamboo skewers. Wrap dough around each sausage. Place on baking sheet.

2 Broil sausages 4 inches from heat source 4 to 6 minutes or until dough is cooked through, turning once. Serve warm with maple syrup for dipping.

Caramelized Bacon

Makes 6 servings

12 slices (about 12 ounces) applewood-smoked bacon
½ cup packed brown sugar

2 tablespoons water
¼ to ½ teaspoon ground red pepper

- -

1 Preheat oven to 375°F. Line 15×10-inch rimmed baking sheet with foil. Spray wire rack with nonstick cooking spray; place on prepared baking sheet.

2 Arrange bacon in single layer on prepared wire rack. Combine brown sugar, water and red pepper in small bowl; mix well. Brush mixture generously over bacon.

3 Bake 20 to 25 minutes or until bacon is well browned and crisp. Immediately remove to serving plate; cool completely.

Note Bacon can be prepared up to 3 days ahead and stored in the refrigerator between sheets of waxed paper in a resealable food storage bag. Let stand at room temperature at least 30 minutes before serving.

Pumpkin Granola

Makes about 5½ cups

3 cups old-fashioned oats
¾ cup coarsely chopped almonds
¾ cup raw pepitas (pumpkin seeds)
½ cup canned pumpkin
½ cup maple syrup
⅓ cup coconut oil, melted or olive oil
1 teaspoon vanilla

1 teaspoon ground cinnamon
½ teaspoon fine salt
¼ teaspoon ground ginger
¼ teaspoon ground nutmeg
Pinch ground cloves
¾ cup dried cranberries
Flaky sea salt (optional)

1 Preheat oven to 325°F. Line large rimmed baking sheet with parchment paper.

2 Combine oats, almonds and pepitas in large bowl; mix well. Whisk pumpkin, maple syrup, oil, vanilla, cinnamon, ½ teaspoon salt, ginger, nutmeg and cloves in medium bowl until well blended. Pour over oat mixture; stir until well blended and all ingredients are completely coated. Spread evenly on prepared baking sheet.

3 Bake 50 to 60 minutes or until granola is golden brown and no longer moist, stirring every 20 minutes. (Granola will become more crisp as it cools.) Stir in cranberries and season with flaky salt, if desired; cool completely.

Bacon Waffles with Maple Cream
Makes 9 to 10 waffles

Maple Cream

1 cup whipping cream
¼ cup maple syrup

Waffles

1 package (about 15 ounces) butter-recipe yellow cake mix
1¼ cups buttermilk*
3 eggs

½ cup (1 stick) butter, melted and cooled
¼ cup maple syrup
1 pound maple bacon, crisp-cooked and finely chopped

*If buttermilk is unavailable, substitute 3½ teaspoons vinegar or lemon juice and enough milk to equal 1¼ cups. Let stand 5 minutes.

1 For Maple Cream, whip cream and ¼ cup maple syrup in medium bowl with electric mixer fitted with whisk attachment at high speed until soft peaks form. Refrigerate until ready to serve.

2 Preheat oven to 200°F. Place wire rack on baking sheet; place in oven. Preheat waffle maker according to manufacturer's directions. Spray cooking surface with nonstick cooking spray.

3 Combine cake mix, buttermilk, eggs, butter and ¼ cup maple syrup in large bowl. Add bacon; mix well. Spoon batter by ½ cupfuls onto heated waffle maker (batter will be thick). Cook 4 minutes or until steaming stops and waffles are lightly browned. Keep warm on wire rack in oven. Repeat with remaining batter. Serve with Maple Cream.

Irish Porridge with Berry Compote

Makes 4 servings

4 cups plus 1 tablespoon water, divided

1 teaspoon fine salt

1 cup steel-cut oats

½ teaspoon ground cinnamon

⅓ cup half-and-half

¼ cup packed brown sugar

1 cup fresh strawberries, hulled and quartered

1 container (6 ounces) fresh blackberries

1 container (6 ounces) fresh blueberries

3 tablespoons granulated sugar

Flaky sea salt

----

1 Bring 4 cups water and 1 teaspoon salt to a boil in medium saucepan over medium-high heat. Whisk in oats and cinnamon. Reduce heat to medium; simmer, uncovered, about 40 minutes or until water is absorbed and oats are tender. Remove from heat; stir in half-and-half and brown sugar.

2 Meanwhile, combine strawberries, blackberries, blueberries, granulated sugar and remaining 1 tablespoon water in small saucepan; bring to a simmer over medium heat. Cook about 10 minutes or until berries are tender but still hold their shape, stirring occasionally.

3 Divide porridge among four bowls; top with berry compote and flaky salt.

Sweet Potato & Turkey Sausage Hash
Makes 2 to 4 servings

1 Italian sausage link (about
    4 ounces)
1 tablespoon vegetable oil
1 red onion, finely chopped
1 red bell pepper, finely chopped
1 sweet potato, peeled and cut into
    ½-inch cubes

¼ teaspoon salt
¼ teaspoon black pepper
⅛ teaspoon ground cumin
⅛ teaspoon chipotle chili powder

----

1 Remove sausage from casing; shape sausage into ½-inch balls. Spray large nonstick skillet with nonstick cooking spray; heat over medium heat. Add sausage; cook and stir 3 to 5 minutes or until browned. Remove to plate.

2 Heat oil in same skillet over medium-high heat. Add onion, bell pepper, sweet potato, salt, black pepper, cumin and chili powder; cook and stir 5 to 8 minutes or until sweet potato is tender.

3 Stir in sausage; cook without stirring 5 minutes or until hash is lightly browned on bottom.

Cranberry Walnut Granola Bars
Makes 12 bars

2 packages (3 ounces each) ramen noodles,* broken into small pieces

¾ cup all-purpose flour

1 teaspoon pumpkin pie spice

½ teaspoon baking soda

½ teaspoon salt

1 cup packed brown sugar

¼ cup (½ stick) butter, softened

2 eggs

¼ cup orange juice

1 cup chopped walnuts

½ cup dried cranberries

Use any flavor; discard seasoning packets.

1 Preheat oven to 350°F. Spray 9-inch square baking pan with nonstick cooking spray.

2 Combine noodles, flour, pumpkin pie spice, baking soda and salt in medium bowl.

3 Beat brown sugar and butter in large bowl with electric mixer at medium-high speed until light and fluffy. Add eggs and orange juice; beat until blended. Gradually add noodle mixture at low speed, beating just until blended. Stir in walnuts and cranberries. Spread batter in prepared pan.

4 Bake 20 to 25 minutes or until toothpick inserted into center comes out clean. Cool completely in pan on wire rack; cut into bars.

Bacon & Maple Grits Puff
Makes 6 to 8 servings

8 slices bacon
2 cups milk
1¼ cups water
1 cup quick-cooking grits

½ teaspoon salt
½ cup maple syrup
4 eggs
Minced fresh chives (optional)

----

1 Preheat oven to 350°F. Grease 1½-quart soufflé dish or round casserole.

2 Cook bacon in large skillet over medium-high heat until crisp. Drain on paper towels; set aside. Reserve 2 tablespoons bacon fat.

3 Bring milk, water, grits and salt to a boil in medium saucepan over medium heat, stirring frequently. Reduce heat to low; simmer 2 minutes or until mixture thickens, stirring constantly. Remove from heat; stir in maple syrup and reserved 2 tablespoons bacon fat.

4 Crumble bacon; reserve ¼ cup for garnish. Stir remaining crumbled bacon into grits mixture.

5 Beat eggs in medium bowl with electric mixer at high speed until thick and pale yellow. Stir spoonful of grits mixture into eggs until well blended. Fold egg mixture into remaining grits mixture until blended. Spoon into prepared dish.

6 Bake 1 hour 20 minutes or until knife inserted into center comes out clean. Top with reserved ¼ cup bacon and chives, if desired. Serve immediately.

Note Puff will fall slightly after being removed from oven.

Peanut Butter & Jelly French Toast
Makes 6 pieces

1 banana, sliced
2 tablespoons peanuts, chopped
2 tablespoons orange juice
1 tablespoon honey
6 slices whole wheat bread

¼ cup grape jelly, or favorite flavor
¼ cup creamy peanut butter
2 eggs
¼ cup milk
2 tablespoons butter

----

1 Combine banana, peanuts, orange juice and honey in small bowl. Spread three bread slices with jelly and three slices with peanut butter. Press peanut butter and jelly slices together to form three sandwiches; cut each sandwich in half diagonally.

2 Beat eggs and milk in shallow bowl. Dip sandwiches in egg mixture, turning to coat.

3 Melt butter on large nonstick griddle or skillet over medium-high heat. Cook sandwiches 2 minutes per side or until lightly browned. Top with banana mixture.

Cherry Oatmeal
Makes 4 servings

3 cups water
1 cup milk
1 teaspoon salt
3 cups old-fashioned oats

½ cup dried cherries
⅓ cup packed dark brown sugar
Whipping cream or half-and-half

1 Bring water, milk and salt to a boil in large saucepan over high heat. Stir in oats, cherries and brown sugar.

2 Reduce heat to medium; cook 4 to 5 minutes or until thick and creamy, stirring frequently. Serve with cream.

Sweet & Savory Breakfast Muffins

Makes 12 muffins

1¼ cups original pancake and baking mix

1 cup milk

3 egg whites

¼ cup maple syrup

4 small fully cooked breakfast sausage links, diced

1 cup fresh blueberries

---

1 Preheat oven to 375°F. Spray 12 standard (2½-inch) muffin cups with nonstick cooking spray.

2 Combine pancake mix, milk, egg whites and maple syrup in large bowl; stir until smooth and well blended. Fold in sausage and blueberries. Divide batter evenly among prepared muffin cups.

3 Bake 18 to 20 minutes or until toothpick inserted into centers comes out clean. Serve warm.

Hawaiian Breakfast Pizza
Makes 1 serving

2 teaspoons pineapple jam or
   barbecue sauce
1 English muffin, split and toasted
1 slice (1 ounce) smoked ham, diced

½ cup pineapple tidbits, drained
2 tablespoons shredded Cheddar
   cheese

1 Preheat toaster oven. Spread jam over each muffin half; place on foil-lined toaster oven tray. Sprinkle ham and pineapple over muffin halves; top with cheese.

2 Toast 2 minutes or until cheese is melted.

Note To heat in a conventional oven, preheat oven to 400°F. Bake muffin halves on a foil-lined baking sheet and bake 5 minutes or until cheese is melted.

Appetizers

Goat Cheese-Stuffed Figs
Makes 14 pieces

7 fresh firm ripe figs
7 slices prosciutto

1 package (4 ounces) goat cheese
Black pepper

----

1 Preheat broiler. Line baking sheet with foil. Cut figs in half vertically. Cut prosciutto slices in half lengthwise to create 14 pieces (about 4 inches long and 1 inch wide).

2 Spread 1 teaspoon goat cheese onto cut side of each fig half. Wrap prosciutto slice around fig and goat cheese. Sprinkle with pepper.

3 Broil about 4 minutes or until cheese softens and figs are heated through.

Raspberry-Balsamic Glazed Meatballs

Makes about 32 meatballs

1 bag (32 ounces) frozen fully cooked meatballs

1 cup raspberry preserves

3 tablespoons sugar

3 tablespoons balsamic vinegar

1 tablespoon plus 1½ teaspoons Worcestershire sauce

¼ teaspoon red pepper flakes

1 tablespoon grated fresh ginger (optional)

Slow Cooker Directions

1 Coat inside of slow cooker with nonstick cooking spray. Add meatballs.

2 Combine preserves, sugar, vinegar, Worcestershire sauce and red pepper flakes in small microwavable bowl. Microwave on HIGH 45 seconds; stir. Microwave 15 seconds or until melted. Reserve ½ cup preserves mixture. Pour remaining mixture over meatballs; toss to coat. Cover; cook on LOW 5 hours or on HIGH 2½ hours.

3 Stir in ginger, if desired, and reserved ½ cup preserves mixture. Cook, uncovered, on HIGH 15 to 20 minutes or until thickened slightly, stirring occasionally.

Crunchy Cheddar Ball
with Strawberry-Pepper Sauce
Makes 2 cups

1 package (3 ounces) ramen noodles, crushed*

1 package (8 ounces) cream cheese, softened

1 cup (4 ounces) finely shredded sharp Cheddar cheese

¼ cup mayonnaise

3 tablespoons finely chopped green onion

1 tablespoon Dijon mustard

½ teaspoon Worcestershire sauce

½ teaspoon curry powder

¾ cup chopped pecans, toasted**

½ cup strawberry preserves

1 jalapeño pepper, seeded and minced

1 teaspoon balsamic vinegar

Assorted crackers

Apple and/or pear slices

Use any flavor; discard seasoning packet.

**To toast pecans, cook and stir in small skillet over medium-low heat 2 to 3 minutes or until fragrant.*

----

1 Combine noodles, cream cheese, Cheddar cheese, mayonnaise, green onion, mustard, Worcestershire sauce and curry powder in food processor; process until well blended. With dampened hands, shape cheese mixture into a ball. Wrap in plastic wrap and refrigerate 1 hour to allow flavors to blend.

2 For sauce, combine preserves, jalapeño and vinegar in small saucepan. Cook and stir over medium heat 3 minutes or until well blended and hot. Transfer to bowl; cover and refrigerate 30 minutes.

3 Spread pecans in shallow bowl. Roll cheese ball in nuts to coat. Place on serving plate; serve with sauce, crackers and fruit slices.

Goat Cheese Crostini with Sweet Onion Jam

Makes 24 crostini

1 tablespoon olive oil

2 medium yellow onions, thinly sliced

¾ cup dry red wine

¼ cup water

2 tablespoons packed brown sugar

1 tablespoon balsamic vinegar

1 teaspoon salt

¼ teaspoon black pepper

2 ounces soft goat cheese

2 ounces cream cheese, softened

1 teaspoon chopped fresh thyme, plus additional for garnish

1 loaf (16 ounces) French bread, cut into 24 slices (about 1 inch thick), lightly toasted

1 Heat oil in large skillet over medium heat. Add onions; cook and stir 10 minutes. Add wine, water, brown sugar, vinegar, salt and pepper; bring to a simmer. Reduce heat to low. Cook 15 to 20 minutes or until all liquid is absorbed, stirring occasionally. (If mixture appears dry, stir in additional water by tablespoonfuls.) Cool 30 minutes or cover and refrigerate until ready to use.

2 Stir goat cheese, cream cheese and 1 teaspoon thyme in small bowl until well blended. Spread goat cheese mixture on bread slices; top with onion jam. Garnish with additional thyme.

Sweet Hot Chicken Wings

Makes about 36 wings

3 pounds chicken wings

¾ cup spicy salsa

⅔ cup honey

⅓ cup soy sauce

¼ cup Dijon mustard

2 tablespoons vegetable oil

1 tablespoon grated fresh ginger

½ teaspoon grated orange peel

½ teaspoon grated lemon peel

Blue cheese or ranch dressing (optional)

1 Cut off and discard wing tips from chicken. Cut each wing in half at joint. Place wings in 13×9-inch baking dish.

2 Combine salsa, honey, soy sauce, mustard, oil, ginger, orange peel and lemon peel in medium bowl; mix well. Pour over wings. Cover and marinate in refrigerator 6 hours or overnight.

3 Preheat oven to 400°F. Line large baking sheet with foil. Place wings in single layer on prepared baking sheet. Pour marinade evenly over wings. Bake 40 to 45 minutes until browned and cooked through. Serve warm with blue cheese dressing, if desired.

Apricot Brie en Croûte
Makes 6 servings

1 sheet frozen puff pastry (half of 17¼-ounce package)

1 round Brie cheese (8 ounces)
¼ cup apricot preserves

----

1 Unfold puff pastry; thaw 20 minutes on lightly floured surface. Preheat oven to 400°F. Line baking sheet with parchment paper.

2 Roll out puff pastry to 12-inch square. Place cheese in center of square; spread preserves over top of cheese.

3 Gather up edges of puff pastry; bring together over center of cheese, covering entirely. Pinch and twist pastry edges together to seal. Transfer to prepared baking sheet.

4 Bake 20 to 25 minutes or until golden brown. (If top of pastry browns too quickly, cover loosely with small piece of foil.) Cut into wedges; serve warm.

Variation For added flavor and texture, sprinkle 2 tablespoons sliced almonds over the preserves. Proceed with wrapping and baking the Brie as directed.

Fig, Bacon & Blue Cheese Pizza

Makes 8 to 10 appetizer servings

1 (12-inch) prepared pizza crust

2 tablespoons olive oil, divided

1 red onion, thinly sliced

½ cup (2 ounces) shredded Monterey Jack cheese

3 tablespoons fig jam

4 slices turkey bacon or regular bacon, crisp-cooked and coarsely chopped

⅓ cup sliced dried figs

½ cup crumbled gorgonzola cheese

2 tablespoons balsamic glaze

Baby arugula (optional)

---

1 Preheat oven to 450°F. Place pizza crust on baking sheet or pizza pan. Brush with 1 tablespoon oil.

2 Heat remaining 1 tablespoon oil in large skillet over medium heat. Add onion; cook and stir 10 minutes or until soft and browned. Spread over pizza crust; sprinkle with Monterey Jack cheese. Dot with jam and top with bacon and figs. Sprinkle with gorgonzola cheese.

3 Bake about 10 minutes or until crust is lightly browned and cheese is melted. Drizzle balsamic glaze over pizza; top with arugula, if desired. Cut into wedges or squares to serve.

Apricot Chicken Pot Stickers
Makes 30 pot stickers

Sweet & Sour Sauce (page 39)

2 cups plus 1 tablespoon water, divided

8 ounces boneless skinless chicken breasts

1 teaspoon salt

2 cups chopped finely shredded cabbage

½ cup apricot fruit spread

2 green onions, finely chopped

2 teaspoons soy sauce

½ teaspoon grated fresh ginger

⅛ teaspoon black pepper

30 (3-inch) wonton wrappers

- -

1 Prepare Sweet & Sour Sauce; set aside.

2 Bring 2 cups water to a boil in medium saucepan. Add chicken and salt. Reduce heat to low; cover and simmer 10 minutes or until chicken is cooked through (165°). Drain and place on cutting board; cool slightly. Finely chop when cool enough to handle.

3 Combine cabbage and remaining 1 tablespoon water in same saucepan; cook over high heat 1 to 2 minutes or until water is evaporated, stirring occasionally. Remove from heat; cool slightly. Stir in chicken, fruit spread, green onions, soy sauce, ginger and pepper; mix well.

4 Place one wonton wrapper on work surface. Place slightly rounded tablespoonful of chicken mixture in center of wrapper; brush edges lightly with water. Bring corners to center; press to seal. Repeat with remaining wrappers and filling.

5 Spray steamer basket with nonstick cooking spray. Place in large saucepan or wok. Add water to depth of about ½ inch below steamer basket not touching steamer. Remove steamer. Cover; bring water to a boil over high heat. Working in batches, if necessary, fill steamer with pot stickers, leaving space between so pot stickers do not touch. Carefully place steamer in saucepan. Cover and steam 5 minutes. Remove to serving plate. Repeat with remaining pot stickers, if necessary. Serve with Sweet & Sour Sauce.

Sweet & Sour Sauce

Makes about 1¼ cups

1 cup apricot fruit spread
¼ cup cider or white vinegar
2 tablespoons packed brown sugar

½ to 1 teaspoon dry mustard
½ teaspoon ground ginger

Combine fruit spread, vinegar, brown sugar, mustard and ginger in small saucepan; cook and stir 2 to 3 minutes over low heat until sugar is melted; remove from heat. Cool completely.

Spicy Korean Chicken Wings

Makes 6 to 8 servings

2 tablespoons peanut oil, plus additional for frying
2 tablespoons grated fresh ginger
½ cup soy sauce
¼ cup cider vinegar
¼ cup honey

¼ cup chili garlic sauce
2 tablespoons orange juice
1 tablespoon toasted sesame oil
18 chicken wings or drummettes
Salt and black pepper
Sesame seeds (optional)

1 Heat 2 tablespoons peanut oil in medium skillet over medium-high heat. Add ginger; cook and stir 1 minute. Add soy sauce, vinegar, honey, chili garlic sauce, orange juice and sesame oil; cook and stir 2 minutes. Pour sauce into large bowl.

2 Heat 2 inches of peanut oil in large heavy saucepan over medium-high heat to 350° to 375°F; adjust heat to maintain temperature during frying.

3 Remove and discard wing tips. Season wings all over with salt and pepper.

4 Add wings to oil and cook 8 to 10 minutes or until crispy and browned and chicken is cooked through. Remove to paper towel-lined plate to drain.

5 Add wings to sauce; toss to coat. Sprinkle with sesame seeds, if desired.

Spicy BBQ Party Franks
Makes 6 to 8 servings

1 tablespoon butter
1 package (1 pound) cocktail franks
⅓ cup cola beverage
⅓ cup ketchup

2 tablespoons hot pepper sauce
2 tablespoons packed dark brown sugar
1 tablespoon cider vinegar

1 Melt butter in large skillet over medium heat. Pierce cocktail franks with fork. Add franks to skillet; cook and stir until lightly browned.

2 Stir in cola, ketchup, hot pepper sauce, brown sugar and vinegar. Reduce heat to low; cook until sauce is reduced to sticky glaze.

Sweet & Spicy Sausage Rounds

Makes about 16 servings

1 pound kielbasa sausage, cut into
¼-inch-thick rounds

⅔ cup blackberry jam

⅓ cup steak sauce

1 tablespoon yellow mustard

½ teaspoon ground allspice

- -

Slow Cooker Directions

1 Combine sausage, jam, steak sauce, mustard and allspice in slow cooker; mix well.

2 Cover; cook on HIGH 3 hours. Remove sausage to serving bowl using slotted spoon.

Maple-Glazed Meatballs

Makes about 48 meatballs

2 packages (about 16 ounces each) frozen fully cooked meatballs, partially thawed and separated

1 can (20 ounces) pineapple chunks in juice, drained

1½ cups ketchup

1 cup maple syrup

⅓ cup soy sauce

1 tablespoon quick-cooking tapioca

1 teaspoon dry mustard

½ teaspoon ground allspice

- -

Slow Cooker Directions

1 Combine meatballs, pineapple, ketchup, maple syrup, soy sauce, tapioca, mustard and allspice in slow cooker; mix well.

2 Cover; cook on LOW 5 to 6 hours. Stir before serving.

Honey Nut Brie
Makes 16 to 20 servings

¼ cup honey
¼ cup coarsely chopped pecans
1 tablespoon brandy (optional)

1 wheel (14 ounces) Brie cheese
(about 5-inch diameter)
Crackers, apple slices and grapes

1 Preheat oven to 450°F. Combine honey, pecans and brandy, if desired, in small bowl. Place cheese on ovenproof serving plate or in 9-inch pie plate.

2 Bake 4 to 5 minutes or until cheese softens. Drizzle honey mixture over top of cheese. Bake 2 to 3 minutes longer or until topping is thoroughly heated. *Do not melt cheese.* Serve with crackers and fruit.

Salads

Toasted Peanut Couscous Salad
Makes 4 servings

½ cup water
¾ teaspoon salt, divided
¼ cup uncooked couscous
½ cup finely chopped red onion
½ cup finely chopped green bell
  pepper
1 ounce dry-roasted peanuts

1 tablespoon soy sauce
1 tablespoon sugar
2 teaspoons cider vinegar
1½ teaspoons toasted sesame oil
½ teaspoon grated fresh ginger
⅛ teaspoon red pepper flakes

1 Bring water and ½ teaspoon salt to a boil in small saucepan over high heat.
   Remove from heat; stir in couscous. Cover and let stand 5 minutes or until
   water is absorbed. Place couscous in medium bowl; fluff with fork and cool slightly.
   Stir in onion and bell pepper.

2 Heat small nonstick skillet over medium-high heat until hot. Add peanuts; cook
   2 to 3 minutes or until beginning to turn golden, stirring frequently. Add to
   couscous.

3 Whisk soy sauce, sugar, vinegar, oil, ginger, remaining ¼ teaspoon salt and red
   pepper flakes in small bowl. Add to couscous; stir until well blended.

Chicken Waldorf Salad
Makes 4 servings

Dressing

⅔ cup extra virgin olive oil

⅓ cup balsamic vinegar

2 tablespoons Dijon mustard

2 teaspoons minced garlic

½ teaspoon salt

¼ teaspoon black pepper

Salad

8 cups mixed greens

1 large Granny Smith apple, cut into ½-inch pieces

⅔ cup diced celery

⅔ cup halved red seedless grapes

1 package (16 ounces) grilled chicken breast strips

½ cup candied walnuts*

½ cup crumbled blue cheese

*Candied or glazed walnuts may found in the produce section of the supermarket with other salad toppings, or in the snack aisle.

1 For dressing, whisk oil, vinegar, mustard, garlic, salt and pepper in medium bowl until blended.

2 For salad, combine mixed greens, apple, celery and grapes in large bowl. Add half of dressing; toss to coat. Top with chicken, walnuts and cheese; drizzle with additional dressing.

Cold Peanut Noodle & Edamame Salad

Makes 4 servings

½ (8-ounce) package brown rice pad thai noodles

3 tablespoons soy sauce

2 tablespoons toasted sesame oil

2 tablespoons unseasoned rice vinegar

1 tablespoon sugar

1 tablespoon grated fresh ginger

1 tablespoon creamy peanut butter

1 tablespoon sriracha or hot chili sauce

2 teaspoons minced garlic

½ cup thawed frozen shelled edamame

¼ cup shredded carrots

¼ cup sliced green onions

Chopped peanuts (optional)

----

1 Prepare noodles according to package directions for pasta. Rinse under cold water; drain. Cut noodles into 3-inch lengths; place in large bowl.

2 Whisk soy sauce, oil, vinegar, sugar, ginger, peanut butter, sriracha and garlic in small bowl until smooth and well blended.

3 Pour dressing over noodles; toss gently to coat. Stir in edamame and carrots. Cover and refrigerate at least 30 minutes before serving. Top with green onions and peanuts, if desired.

Note Brown rice pad thai noodles can be found in the Asian section of the supermarket. Regular thin rice noodles or linguine may be substituted.

Pear Arugula Salad
Makes 4 servings

Caramelized Pecans

½ cup pecan halves

3 tablespoons packed brown sugar

1 tablespoon butter

1 tablespoon honey

¼ teaspoon salt

⅛ teaspoon ground cinnamon

Dressing

¼ cup extra virgin olive oil

3 tablespoons balsamic vinegar

1 teaspoon pomegranate molasses or honey

1 teaspoon Dijon mustard

½ teaspoon salt

¼ teaspoon dried thyme

⅛ teaspoon black pepper

Salad

2 cups arugula

2 red pears, thinly sliced

½ cup crumbled gorgonzola, blue or goat cheese

----

1 For pecans, preheat oven to 350°F. Line small baking sheet with foil; spray foil with nonstick cooking spray. Combine pecans, brown sugar, butter, honey, ¼ teaspoon salt and cinnamon in medium skillet. Cook and stir 2 to 3 minutes or until sugar and butter are melted and nuts are glazed. Spread on foil. Bake 5 to 7 minutes or until nuts are fragrant and a shade darker. Remove foil from baking sheet; cool nuts completely on foil.

2 For dressing, whisk oil, vinegar, molasses, mustard, ½ teaspoon salt, thyme and pepper in small bowl until smooth and well blended.

3 Divide arugula among four bowls or plates. Top with pears, nuts and cheese; drizzle with 2 tablespoons dressing.

Strawberry Poppy Seed Chicken Salad
Makes 4 servings

Dressing

- ¼ cup white wine vinegar
- 2 tablespoons orange juice
- 1 tablespoon sugar
- 2 teaspoons poppy seeds
- 1½ teaspoons Dijon mustard
- ½ teaspoon salt
- ½ teaspoon minced dried onion
- ½ cup vegetable oil

Salad

- 8 cups chopped romaine lettuce
- 1 package (16 ounces) grilled chicken breast strips
- ¾ cup fresh pineapple chunks
- ¾ cup sliced fresh strawberries
- ¾ cup fresh blueberries
- 1 navel orange, peeled and sectioned *or* 1 can (11 ounces) mandarin oranges, drained
- ¼ cup chopped toasted pecans

1 For dressing, whisk vinegar, orange juice, sugar, poppy seeds, mustard, salt and dried onion in small bowl until blended. Whisk in oil in thin, steady stream until well blended.

2 For salad, combine romaine and two thirds of dressing in large bowl; toss gently to coat. Divide salad among four plates, top with chicken, pineapple, strawberries, blueberries, oranges and pecans. Serve with remaining dressing.

Crunchy Kale Salad
Makes 6 servings

¼ cup cider vinegar
¼ cup extra virgin olive oil
¼ cup maple syrup
 1 tablespoon lemon juice
½ tablespoon Dijon mustard
½ teaspoon salt
¼ teaspoon black pepper

10 cups chopped stemmed kale (about 1 large bunch)
 2 cups shredded green cabbage
½ cup sliced almonds, toasted*

*To toast almonds, cook and stir in small skillet over medium-low heat 2 to 3 minutes or until fragrant.

1 Whisk vinegar, oil, maple syrup, lemon juice, mustard, salt and pepper in small bowl or measuring cup until well blended.

2 Combine kale and cabbage in large bowl. Pour dressing over vegetables; massage kale with hands 3 to 4 minutes to soften.

3 Stir in almonds just before serving.

Autumn Harvest Salad

Makes 4 to 6 servings

Dressing

- ½ cup extra virgin olive oil
- 3 tablespoons balsamic vinegar
- 1 clove garlic, minced
- 1 teaspoon honey
- 1 teaspoon Dijon mustard
- ½ teaspoon dried oregano
- ½ teaspoon salt
- ⅛ teaspoon black pepper

Salad

- 1 loaf (12 to 16 ounces) artisan pecan raisin bread
- ¼ cup (½ stick) butter, melted
- 6 tablespoons coarse sugar (such as demerara or turbinado)
- 6 cups packed spring greens
- 2 Granny Smith apples, thinly sliced
- 1 package (16 ounces) grilled chicken breast strips
- ¾ cup crumbled blue cheese
- ¾ cup dried cranberries
- ¾ cup toasted walnuts

1 For dressing, whisk oil, vinegar, garlic, honey, mustard, oregano, salt and pepper in medium bowl until well blended. Refrigerate until ready to use.

2 Preheat oven to 350°F. Line baking sheet with parchment paper. Cut bread into thin (¼-inch) slices; place in single layer on prepared baking sheet. Brush one side of each slice with melted butter; sprinkle each slice with ½ teaspoon sugar. Bake 10 minutes. Turn slices; brush with remaining butter and sprinkle with remaining sugar. Bake 10 minutes. Cool completely on baking sheet.

3 Place greens on serving plates; top with apples, chicken, cheese, cranberries and walnuts. Break toast slices into pieces and sprinkle over salads. Drizzle with dressing.

Dinners

Sweet Potato Noodles with Blue Cheese & Walnuts

Makes 2 servings

2 sweet potatoes (1½ to 2 pounds)
¼ cup chopped walnuts
1 tablespoon olive oil
2 cloves garlic, minced
¼ cup whipping cream

1 package (5 ounces) baby spinach
¼ teaspoon salt
¼ teaspoon black pepper
¼ cup crumbled blue cheese

1 Spiral sweet potatoes with thin ribbon blade of spiralizer. Loosely pile on cutting board and cut in an X.

2 Cook walnuts in large nonstick skillet over medium-high heat 3 to 4 minutes or until toasted, stirring frequently. Remove to plate; cool completely.

3 Heat oil in same skillet over medium-high heat. Add potatoes; cook and stir 10 minutes or until potatoes are desired doneness, adding water by tablespoonfuls if potatoes are browning too quickly.

4 Add garlic to skillet; cook and stir 30 seconds. Add cream, spinach, salt and pepper; cook and stir 1 minute or until cream is absorbed and spinach is wilted. Transfer to bowls; top with walnuts and cheese.

Baked Ham with Sweet & Spicy Glaze
Makes 8 to 10 servings

1 bone-in smoked half ham
  (8 pounds)
¾ cup packed brown sugar
⅓ cup cider vinegar
¼ cup golden raisins
1 can (8½ ounces) sliced peaches in
  heavy syrup, drained, chopped
  and syrup reserved

1 tablespoon cornstarch
¼ cup orange juice
1 can (8¼ ounces) crushed pineapple
  in syrup, undrained
1 tablespoon grated orange peel
1 clove garlic, minced
½ teaspoon red pepper flakes
½ teaspoon grated fresh ginger

1 Preheat oven to 325°F. Place ham, fat side up, in roasting pan. Bake 3 hours.

2 Combine brown sugar, vinegar, raisins and peach syrup in medium saucepan. Bring to a boil over high heat. Reduce heat to low; simmer 8 to 10 minutes.

3 Whisk cornstarch into orange juice in small bowl until smooth and well blended; stir into saucepan. Stir in peaches, pineapple, orange peel, garlic, red pepper flakes and ginger; bring to a boil over medium heat. Cook until sauce is thickened, stirring constantly.

4 Remove ham from oven. Generously brush half of glaze over ham and arrange some of fruit on top; bake 30 minutes or until thermometer inserted into thickest part of ham registers 160°F.

5 Remove ham from oven; brush with remaining glaze. Let stand 20 minutes before slicing.

Sweet Potato Maki Bowl

Makes 4 servings

2 tablespoons vegetable oil, divided
1 large sweet potato (1 pound), peeled
½ cup panko bread crumbs
½ teaspoon salt, divided
⅛ teaspoon ground red pepper
⅓ cup water
¼ cup cornstarch
1 cup Calrose rice, sushi rice or other short grain rice

1 tablespoon rice vinegar
1 teaspoon granulated sugar
½ cup soy sauce
1 tablespoon packed brown sugar
¼ cup mayonnaise
1 tablespoon sriracha sauce
½ cucumber, cut in half lengthwise and thinly sliced crosswise
1 avocado, cubed
Sesame seeds

1 Preheat oven to 400°F. Line baking sheet with foil; brush with 1 tablespoon oil.

2 Cut sweet potato in half lengthwise; cut crosswise into ¼-inch slices. Combine panko, ¼ teaspoon salt and red pepper in shallow bowl. Combine ⅓ cup water, cornstarch and remaining ¼ teaspoon salt in another shallow bowl; mix until smooth. Dip sweet potato slices in cornstarch mixture, letting excess drip back into bowl. Roll in panko mixture to coat; place on prepared baking sheet.

3 Bake 20 to 25 minutes or until potatoes are tender and coating is golden brown, turning once.

4 Meanwhile, cook rice according to package directions. Stir vinegar and granulated sugar into cooked rice.

5 Combine soy sauce and brown sugar in small saucepan; cook over low heat until mixture is reduced and syrupy. Combine mayonnaise and sriracha in small bowl.

6 Divide rice among serving bowls. Top with sweet potatoes, cucumber and avocado; drizzle with soy sauce mixture and sprinkle with sesame seeds. Serve with sriracha mayonnaise.

Chicken Mirabella
Makes 4 servings

4 boneless skinless chicken breasts
    (6 to 8 ounces each)
½ cup pitted prunes
½ cup assorted pitted olives (black,
    green and/or a combination)
¼ cup dry white wine
2 tablespoons olive oil

1 tablespoon drained capers
1 tablespoon red wine vinegar
1 teaspoon dried oregano
1 clove garlic, minced
1 tablespoon chopped fresh parsley
1 tablespoon packed brown sugar

1 Preheat oven to 350°F.

2 Place chicken in 8-inch baking dish. Combine prunes, olives, wine, oil, capers, vinegar, oregano, garlic and parsley in medium bowl. Pour evenly over chicken. Sprinkle with brown sugar.

3 Bake 25 to 30 minutes or until chicken is cooked through (165°F), basting with sauce halfway through cooking.

Tip For more intense flavor, marinate chicken in olive mixture in baking dish 8 hours or overnight. Sprinkle with brown sugar just before baking.

Thai Rama with Tofu

Makes 4 servings

1 cup uncooked medium or short grain rice

2 heads broccoli (about 1½ pounds), cut into florets

1 package (14 to 16 ounces) firm or extra firm tofu, drained

Salt and black pepper

½ cup plus 1 tablespoon cornstarch, divided

3 tablespoons plus 2 teaspoons vegetable oil, divided

½ cup finely chopped onion

3 cloves garlic, minced

½ cup creamy peanut butter

3 tablespoons packed brown sugar

2 tablespoons soy sauce

1 teaspoon paprika

¼ teaspoon ground red pepper

1 cup unsweetened coconut milk

1 tablespoon water, plus more if needed

2 tablespoons lime juice

1 Cook rice according to package directions; cover and let stand until ready to serve. Bring large saucepan of water to a boil. Add broccoli; cook 4 minutes or until tender. Drain and set aside.

2 For tofu, stand tofu on long short end and cut into four slices. Turn onto large flat side; cut into quarters lengthwise, then cut in half crosswise to make 32 thin rectangles. Place in single layer on cutting board; press gently with paper towels to remove excess moisture. Season tofu with salt and pepper. Place ½ cup cornstarch in medium bowl. Add tofu to cornstarch in batches; toss gently to coat. Heat 2 tablespoons oil in large nonstick skillet over medium-high heat. Working in batches, cook tofu in single layer about 5 minutes per side or until lightly browned, adding additional 1 tablespoon oil as needed.

3 Meanwhile for sauce, heat remaining 2 teaspoons oil in medium saucepan over medium-high heat. Add onion and garlic; cook and stir 2 to 3 minutes or until tender. Reduce heat to medium; stir in peanut butter, brown sugar, soy sauce, paprika and red pepper until smooth. Slowly stir in coconut milk until well blended. Bring to a simmer. Stir 1 tablespoon water into remaining 1 tablespoon cornstarch

in small bowl until smooth; stir into sauce. Cook and stir 1 to 2 minutes or until sauce is thickened. Stir in lime juice.

4 Return all tofu to skillet. Pour in sauce; cook and stir over medium heat until tofu is coated, adding additional water by tablespoonfuls if sauce is too thick. Serve with rice and broccoli.

Pumpkin Ravioli
Makes 4 servings

½ cup canned pumpkin
2 teaspoons packed brown sugar
¼ teaspoon salt
¼ teaspoon black pepper
1 package (14 ounces) wonton wrappers

Whole Italian parsley leaves
2 tablespoons olive oil
2 tablespoons butter
2 to 3 cloves garlic, minced
¾ cup shredded Parmesan cheese
2 tablespoons chopped walnuts

1 Combine pumpkin, brown sugar, salt and pepper in medium bowl.

2 Unwrap wontons; cover with plastic wrap. Lay four wontons on work surface. Brush two wontons with water, then place one parsley leaf in center of each wonton. Place another wonton over each parsley leaf, pressing out air and sealing edges. Brush one layered wonton with water, then place 1 teaspoon pumpkin mixture in center of wonton. Top with remaining layered wonton, pressing out air and sealing edges. Repeat with remaining wontons, parsley leaves and pumpkin filling.

3 For circle ravioli, cut filled wontons using 3-inch round cookie cutter. Cover with plastic wrap until ready to cook.

4 Bring large pot of salted water to a boil. Working in batches, slide ravioli into boiling water; cook 1 minute or until ravioli float to surface. Remove with slotted spoon to shallow bowl.

5 Heat oil in large skillet over medium-low heat. Add butter and garlic; cook and stir 1 minute or until garlic is fragrant. Add ravioli; cook over low heat 1 minute or until heated through. Sprinkle with cheese and walnuts; serve immediately.

Coconut Shrimp
Makes 4 servings

Spicy Orange-Mustard Sauce
(recipe follows)

¾ cup all-purpose flour

¾ cup beer or water

1 egg

¾ teaspoon baking powder

½ teaspoon salt

¼ teaspoon ground red pepper

1 cup flaked coconut

2 packages (3 ounces each) ramen
noodles, crushed*

20 jumbo raw shrimp, peeled and
deveined (with tails on)

2 cups vegetable oil

Use any flavor; discard seasoning packets.

1 Prepare Spicy Orange-Mustard Sauce.

2 Whisk flour, beer, egg, baking powder, salt and red pepper in medium bowl. Combine coconut and noodles in another medium bowl. Dip shrimp in batter, letting excess drip back into bowl. Roll in coconut mixture to coat.

3 Heat oil in large skillet to 350°F. Line large plate with paper towels. Working in batches, cook shrimp 3 minutes or just until golden, turning once halfway. Drain on prepared plate. Serve with Spicy Orange-Mustard Sauce.

Spicy Orange-Mustard Sauce Combine ¼ cup coarse grain or Dijon mustard, 2 tablespoons honey, 2 tablespoons orange juice, 2 teaspoons grated orange peel, ½ teaspoon ground red pepper and ¼ teaspoon ground ginger in small bowl; stir until blended.

Spicy Peanut Noodles

Makes 2 to 4 servings

1 package (about 14 ounces) Asian stir-fry wheat noodles (hokkien, udon or chow mein)

3 tablespoons water, plus additional if needed

3 tablespoons soy sauce

2½ tablespoons creamy peanut butter

2 tablespoons unseasoned rice vinegar

1 tablespoon packed brown sugar

1 tablespoon minced fresh cilantro

1 tablespoon hot chili oil

¼ teaspoon red pepper flakes

½ cucumber, peeled and julienned
Fresh cilantro leaves

---

1 Cook noodles according to package directions; drain.

2 Meanwhile, whisk 3 tablespoons water, soy sauce, peanut butter, vinegar, brown sugar, minced cilantro, chili oil and red pepper flakes in large bowl until smooth and well blended. Add noodles; stir until well coated, adding additional water if needed to thin sauce. Cover and refrigerate until cold.

3 Divide noodles among serving bowls; top with cucumber and cilantro.

Note You can substitute 8 ounces uncooked spaghetti or linguine for the Asian stir-fry noodles. Cook the pasta in a large saucepan of salted boiling water according to package directions for al dente. Drain and place in a large serving bowl, reserving some of the pasta cooking water to use in the sauce.

Apricot Brisket

Makes 8 servings

1 cup chopped dried apricots, divided
1 cup canned diced tomatoes, divided
2 teaspoons ground cumin
1 teaspoon salt, divided
1 clove garlic
¼ teaspoon ground cinnamon
1 medium onion, thinly sliced
2 carrots, cut into 1-inch pieces

1 small beef brisket (about 2 to 3 pounds), trimmed of fat
½ teaspoon black pepper
1½ cups beef broth
2 tablespoons cold water
2 tablespoons cornstarch
Chopped fresh parsley (optional)

- -

1 Preheat oven to 325°F.

2 Combine ½ cup chopped apricots, ½ cup tomatoes, cumin, ½ teaspoon salt, garlic and cinnamon in food processor. Pulse until coarsely chopped.

3 Spread onion and carrots in roasting pan. Place brisket on top. Cut several small slits across top of brisket; gently spoon apricot mixture into slits. Sprinkle brisket with remaining ½ teaspoon salt and pepper. Spread remaining ½ cup diced tomatoes over brisket; top with remaining ½ cup apricots. Pour broth over brisket. Cover with foil.

4 Bake brisket 2 to 2½ hours or until very tender. Transfer brisket to carving board; tent with foil and let stand 15 minutes.

5 Pour pan juices and vegetables into medium saucepan. Stir water into cornstarch in small bowl until smooth and well blended. Stir into pan juices; simmer about 5 minutes or until thickened.

6 Carve brisket crosswise into thin slices; serve with onion, carrots, tomatoes, apricots and pan juices. Sprinkle with parsley, if desired.

Peanut Butter Tofu Bowl

Makes 4 servings

Sauce

- ¼ cup creamy peanut butter
- ¼ cup hoisin sauce
- 1 tablespoon packed brown sugar
- 1 tablespoon toasted sesame oil
- 1 tablespoon water
- 1½ teaspoons minced or grated fresh ginger
- 1½ teaspoons unseasoned rice vinegar
- 1½ teaspoons soy sauce
- 1 clove garlic, minced
- ½ teaspoon sriracha sauce

Bowl

- 1 package (14 to 16 ounces) firm tofu, pressed, cut into 24 (1-inch) cubes
- ¼ cup cornstarch
- 2 tablespoons plus 1 teaspoon vegetable oil, divided
- 1 head bok choy
- 1 clove garlic, minced
- 1 tablespoon soy sauce
- 1 tablespoon rice vinegar
- 2 cups hot cooked rice *or* Crispy Rice (page 85)
- Chopped peanuts (optional)

1 For sauce, cook peanut butter, hoisin sauce, brown sugar, sesame oil, 1 tablespoon water, ginger, 1½ teaspoons vinegar, 1½ teaspoons soy sauce, 1 clove garlic and sriracha in small saucepan over medium-low heat 5 minutes, whisking frequently.

2 Toss tofu with cornstarch in large bowl. Heat 2 tablespoons vegetable oil in large nonstick skillet over high heat. Add tofu in single layer; cook without stirring 5 minutes or until well browned and firm on bottom. Turn and cook 5 minutes or until browned on other side. Cook 2 minutes, turning frequently until all sides of tofu are lightly browned. Add sauce; cook 1 minute or until tofu is glazed.

3 Meanwhile, separate leaves and stems of bok choy. Coarsely chop stems and leaves separately. Heat remaining 1 teaspoon vegetable oil in medium skillet over medium-high heat. Add bok choy stems; cook and stir 3 minutes. Add leaves and 1 clove garlic; cook and stir 1 minute. Add 1 tablespoon soy sauce and 1 tablespoon vinegar; cook and stir 30 seconds.

4 Divide tofu, bok choy and rice among bowls. Garnish with peanuts.

Crispy Rice Cook 1 cup long grain rice according to package directions. Stir 1 tablespoon unseasoned rice vinegar, 2 teaspoons sesame seeds and 1 teaspoon granulated sugar into hot rice. Heat 2 tablespoons vegetable oil in medium (10-inch) skillet over medium-high heat. Add rice; pat into even layer. Cook without stirring 10 minutes or until bottom is light brown and crispy (gently lift edge of rice to check doneness). Scoop directly into bowls or invert onto large plate and cut into pieces.

Sweet & Spicy Shrimp Tacos with Mango Salsa
Makes 6 servings

Mango Salsa (recipe follows)
1½ pounds small uncooked shrimp, peeled and deveined
1 teaspoon salt
1 teaspoon granulated sugar
½ cup cola beverage
⅓ cup chili sauce

2 tablespoons packed brown sugar
1 tablespoon lime juice
1 teaspoon hot pepper sauce
1 tablespoon chopped fresh cilantro
6 (6-inch) flour tortillas, warmed or grilled

1   Prepare Mango Salsa.

2   Place shrimp in medium bowl. Sprinkle with salt and granulated sugar; stir to coat. Cover and refrigerate 30 minutes.

3   Meanwhile, bring cola, chili sauce, brown sugar, lime juice and hot pepper sauce to a simmer in small skillet over medium heat; cook until thickened, stirring frequently. Remove from heat; stir in cilantro.

4   Heat large skillet over medium-high heat. Add shrimp; cook and stir 3 minutes or until shrimp are pink and opaque. Remove from heat. Drizzle with sauce; stir until glazed.

5   Serve shrimp in tortillas with Mango Salsa.

Mango Salsa

2 mangoes, pitted and chopped
1 cucumber, peeled, seeded and chopped
1 red or yellow bell pepper, seeded and chopped
1 jalapeño pepper, seeded and finely chopped

¼ cup diced red onion
1 clove garlic, minced
2 tablespoons chopped fresh cilantro
1 tablespoon lime juice
1 tablespoon cola beverage
Salt and black pepper

Combine mangoes, cucumber, bell pepper, jalapeño pepper, onion, garlic, cilantro, lime juice and cola in medium bowl; mix well. Season to taste with salt and pepper. Cover and refrigerate at least 1 hour before serving.

Maple Salmon & Sweet Potatoes
Makes 4 servings

½ cup maple syrup
2 tablespoons butter, melted
1½ pounds skin-on salmon fillets

2 medium sweet potatoes, peeled and cut into ¼-inch slices
1 teaspoon salt
¼ teaspoon black pepper

1 Combine maple syrup and butter in small bowl; mix well. Place salmon in large resealable food storage bag. Place sweet potatoes in another large resealable food storage bag. Pour half of syrup mixture into each bag; seal bags and turn to coat. Refrigerate at least 2 hours or overnight, turning occasionally.

2 Prepare grill for direct cooking. Oil grid. Drain salmon and sweet potatoes; discard marinade. Season with salt and pepper.

3 Grill salmon, skin-side down, on covered grill over medium heat 15 to 20 minutes or until fish begins to flake when tested with fork. (Do not turn.) Grill sweet potatoes, covered, in single layer on grill topper 15 minutes or until tender and lightly browned, turning once or twice.

Sweet & Sour Broccoli Pasta
Makes 4 servings

8 ounces uncooked cavatappi or rotini pasta

2 cups broccoli florets

1 medium Red or Golden Delicious apple, chopped

⅔ cup shredded carrots

⅓ cup plain yogurt

⅓ cup apple juice

3 tablespoons cider vinegar

1 tablespoon olive oil

1 tablespoon Dijon mustard

1 tablespoon honey

½ teaspoon dried thyme

- -

1 Cook pasta in large saucepan of salted boiling water according to package directions for al dente, adding broccoli during last 3 minutes of cooking. Drain and run under cold water until cool. Place in large bowl; stir in apple and carrots.

2 Whisk yogurt, apple juice, vinegar, oil, mustard, honey and thyme in small bowl until smooth and well blended. Pour over pasta mixture; toss to coat.

Japanese Pan Noodles
Makes 2 to 4 servings

⅓ cup soy sauce

⅓ cup packed brown sugar

1 tablespoon mirin

1 teaspoon chili garlic sauce

1 tablespoon vegetable or peanut oil

2 cups small broccoli florets

2 cups sliced mushrooms

1 cup matchstick carrots (about 2 medium) or shredded carrots

1 tablespoon minced or grated fresh ginger

1 package (14 to 16 ounces) cooked udon noodles*

Black sesame seeds

Fresh cilantro sprigs (optional)

Or substitute 1 package (16 ounces) dried or fresh udon noodles; cook and drain according to package directions.

1 Combine soy sauce and brown sugar in small saucepan; bring to a boil over medium-high heat. Reduce heat to medium; cook about 10 minutes or until reduced and thickened slightly, stirring frequently. Remove from heat; stir in mirin and chili garlic sauce.

2 Heat oil in wok or large saucepan over high heat. Add broccoli and mushrooms; cook and stir about 5 minutes or until vegetables are crisp-tender. Add carrots and ginger; cook and stir 1 minute. Add soy sauce mixture and noodles; cook 3 to 5 minutes or until noodles are heated through and most of sauce is absorbed, stirring frequently.

3 Sprinkle with sesame seeds; garnish with cilantro.

Honey Mustard Glazed Chicken
Makes 4 to 5 servings

1 whole chicken (4 to 5 pounds)
1 tablespoon vegetable oil
¼ cup honey
2 tablespoons Dijon mustard

1 tablespoon soy sauce
½ teaspoon ground ginger
⅛ teaspoon black pepper
Dash salt

1. Prepare grill for indirect cooking.

2. Remove giblets from chicken cavity and discard. Pull chicken skin over neck; secure with metal skewer. Tuck wings under back; tie legs together with wet string. Lightly brush chicken with oil.

3. Combine honey, mustard, soy sauce, ginger, pepper and salt in small bowl; set aside.

4. Place chicken, breast side up, on grid directly over drip pan. Grill, covered, over medium-high heat 1 hour 30 minutes or until cooked through (165°F) for both light and dark meat. Brush with glaze every 10 minutes during last 30 minutes of cooking time.*

5. Remove chicken to large cutting board; tent with foil. Let stand 15 minutes before carving. Internal temperature will continue to rise 5°F to 10°F during stand time.

If using grill with heat on one side (rather than around drip pan), rotate chicken 180 degrees after 45 minutes of cooking time.

Sandwiches

Grilled Prosciutto, Brie & Fig Sandwiches

Makes 2 sandwiches

¼ cup fig preserves

4 slices (½ to ¾ inch thick) Italian or
  country bread

  Black pepper

4 to 6 ounces Brie cheese, cut into
  ¼-inch-thick slices

2 slices prosciutto (about half of
  3-ounce package)

¼ cup baby arugula

1½ tablespoons butter

- -

1 Spread preserves over two bread slices. Sprinkle pepper generously over preserves. Top with cheese, prosciutto, arugula and remaining bread slices.

2 Heat medium cast iron skillet over medium heat 5 minutes. Add 1 tablespoon butter; swirl to melt and coat bottom of skillet. Add sandwiches to skillet; cook over medium-low heat about 5 minutes or until bottoms of sandwiches are golden brown.

3 Turn sandwiches and add remaining ½ tablespoon butter to skillet. Tilt pan to melt butter and move sandwiches so butter flows underneath. Cover with foil; cook about 5 minutes or until cheese is melted and bread is golden brown.

Honey-Mustard & Beer Pulled Pork Sandwiches
Makes 8 servings

1 tablespoon chili powder

2 teaspoons ground cumin

1 teaspoon salt

2 tablespoons yellow mustard

4 pounds bone-in pork shoulder roast, cut into two pieces

2 bottles (12 ounces each) beer, divided

¾ cup ketchup

3 tablespoons honey

2 tablespoons cider vinegar

8 hamburger buns or sandwich rolls
   Sliced pickles

1 Prepare grill for indirect cooking over medium-low heat.

2 Combine chili powder, cumin and salt in small bowl. Spread mustard on all sides of pork, then cover evenly with spice mixture. Transfer pork to rack in disposable foil pan. Reserve ¾ cup beer. Pour enough remaining beer into foil pan to just cover rack beneath pork. Place tray on grid opposite heat source.

3 Grill, covered, 4 to 6 hours or until internal temperature reaches 160°F. Remove to cutting board, tent with foil and let stand 15 minutes.

4 Combine reserved ¾ cup beer, ketchup, honey and vinegar in small saucepan. Bring to a boil over medium-high heat. Reduce heat to medium; cook and stir until thickened.

5 Shred pork with two forks, discarding any bone, fat or connective tissue. Combine pork and sauce in medium bowl; stir to coat. Serve on rolls with pickles.

Super Peanut Butter Sandwiches

Makes 4 servings

⅔ cup creamy peanut butter

2 tablespoons toasted wheat germ

1 tablespoon honey

8 slices firm whole wheat or multigrain bread

1 ripe banana, sliced

2 eggs, beaten

⅓ cup orange juice

1 tablespoon grated orange peel

1 tablespoon butter

1 Combine peanut butter, wheat germ and honey in small bowl. Spread evenly on one side of each bread slice.

2 Place banana slices on top of peanut butter mixture on four slices of bread. Top with remaining bread slices, peanut butter side down. Lightly press together.

3 Whisk eggs, orange juice and orange peel in shallow dish. Dip sandwiches in egg mixture, coating both sides.

4 Melt butter in large nonstick skillet over medium heat. Add sandwiches; cook about 3 minutes per side or until golden brown. Serve immediately.

Smokehouse Barbecued Brisket

Makes 6 servings

1 beef brisket, trimmed (3 to 4 pounds)

Salt and black pepper

1 tablespoon garlic powder

3 tablespoons vegetable oil

1 onion, minced

1 tablespoon liquid smoke

1 teaspoon red pepper flakes

2 cups cola beverage, divided

1 cup beef broth

4 tablespoons packed dark brown sugar, divided

1 can (15 ounces) tomato sauce

2 tablespoons onion powder

2 tablespoons hot pepper sauce

1 tablespoon Worcestershire sauce

6 Kaiser rolls or hamburger buns

1 Preheat oven to 300°F. Season brisket generously with salt, black pepper and garlic powder. Heat oil in large skillet over medium-high heat. Add brisket; cook 4 to 5 minutes per side or until well browned. Remove to Dutch oven or covered baking dish.

2 Add onion to skillet; cook and stir over medium-high heat 5 minutes or until softened. Add liquid smoke and red pepper flakes; cook and stir 30 seconds. Add ½ cup cola, stirring to scrape up browned bits. Add broth; bring to a simmer. Pour mixture over meat; sprinkle with 2 tablespoons brown sugar.

3 Bake brisket 5 hours or until meat is falling apart, basting every 30 minutes. Transfer brisket to cutting board; cool slightly.

4 Stir remaining 1½ cups cola, 2 tablespoons brown sugar, tomato sauce, onion powder, hot pepper sauce and Worcestershire sauce into Dutch oven. *Increase heat to 400°F.* Cook, uncovered, 30 minutes.

5 Cut meat across the grain into ½-inch slices. Return brisket to Dutch oven and stir to coat with sauce. *Reduce heat to 250°F.* Cook 30 minutes. Serve on rolls.

Classic Monte Cristo Sandwiches

Makes 4 servings

12 thin slices honey wheat or whole wheat bread
4 ounces sliced deli turkey breast
4 thin slices (2 ounces) Swiss cheese
4 ounces smoked sliced deli ham
4 thin slices (2 ounces) deli American cheese

2 eggs
¼ cup milk
⅛ teaspoon salt
Pinch of ground nutmeg
2 to 3 tablespoons butter
Powdered sugar
Raspberry preserves

1 Preheat oven to 450°F. Line baking sheet with foil.

2 For each sandwich, layer one fourth of turkey and one Swiss cheese slice on one bread slice; top with second bread slice, one fourth of ham, one American cheese slice and third bread slice. Press sandwiches together gently.

3 Beat eggs, milk, salt and nutmeg in shallow dish until blended. Dip both sides of each sandwich briefly in egg mixture, letting excess drip back into dish.

4 Melt 1 tablespoon butter in large nonstick skillet over medium heat. Cook one sandwich at a time 2 to 3 minutes per side or until browned, adding additional butter to skillet as needed. Transfer sandwiches to prepared baking sheet.

5 Bake 5 to 7 minutes or until sandwiches are heated through and cheese is melted. Cut each sandwich in half diagonally; sprinkle with powdered sugar. Serve immediately with raspberry preserves for dipping.

Tip For extra flavor, spread honey mustard on one side of each of three bread slices. Assemble sandwiches as directed above.

Almond Chicken Salad Sandwiches

Makes 4 servings

¼ cup mayonnaise

¼ cup plain Greek yogurt or sour cream

2 tablespoons cider vinegar

1 tablespoon honey

1 teaspoon salt

½ teaspoon black pepper

⅛ teaspoon garlic powder

2 cups chopped cooked chicken

¾ cup halved red grapes

1 stalk celery, chopped

⅓ cup sliced almonds

Leaf lettuce

1 tomato, thinly sliced

8 slices rustic whole grain or country Italian bread

1 Whisk mayonnaise, yogurt, vinegar, honey, salt, pepper and garlic powder in medium bowl until well blended. Add chicken, grapes and celery; mix well.

2 Cover and refrigerate several hours or overnight. Stir in almonds just before serving.

3 Place lettuce and tomato slices on four bread slices; top with chicken salad and remaining bread slices. Serve immediately.

Apple Monte Cristos
Makes 2 sandwiches

1 cup (4 ounces) shredded Gouda
    cheese

1 ounce cream cheese, softened

2 teaspoons honey

½ teaspoon ground cinnamon

4 slices cinnamon raisin bread

1 small apple, cored and thinly sliced

¼ cup milk

1 egg, beaten

1 tablespoon butter

    Powdered sugar

1 Combine Gouda cheese, cream cheese, honey and cinnamon in small bowl; stir until well blended. Spread cheese mixture evenly on all bread slices. Layer apple slices evenly over cheese on two bread slices; top with remaining bread slices.

2 Combine milk and egg in shallow bowl; stir until well blended. Dip both sides of each sandwich in egg mixture.

3 Melt butter in large nonstick skillet over medium heat. Add sandwiches; cook 4 to 5 minutes per side or until cheese is melted and sandwiches are golden brown. Sprinkle with powdered sugar.

Stacked Kaisers with Sweet Spiced Spread

Makes 4 servings

- ¼ cup mayonnaise
- 3 tablespoons prepared yellow mustard
- 1 tablespoon packed dark brown sugar
- 1 teaspoon prepared horseradish
- ⅛ teaspoon ground cinnamon
- 4 Kaiser rolls, cut in half and toasted, if desired
- 6 ounces thinly sliced deli honey-baked ham
- 6 ounces thinly sliced deli smoked turkey
- 4 slices Swiss cheese
- 4 slices American cheese
- 4 thin slices red onion
- 8 green bell pepper rings

1 For spread, combine mayonnaise, mustard, brown sugar, horseradish and cinnamon in small bowl; mix well.

2 Spread cut sides of each roll with about 1 tablespoon spread. Arrange ham, turkey, Swiss and American cheeses, onion and bell pepper on bottoms of rolls. Top with tops of rolls; press down gently.

Cherry & Cheese Panini
Makes 4 servings

1 tablespoon olive oil

1 large red onion, thinly sliced

¼ teaspoon dried thyme

2 teaspoons balsamic vinegar

⅛ teaspoon salt

⅛ teaspoon black pepper

½ cup fresh sweet cherries, pitted and chopped

4 ounces blue cheese, at room temperature

3 ounces cream cheese, softened

8 large thin slices Italian or country-style bread

1 to 2 tablespoons butter

- -

1 Heat oil in large heavy skillet over medium heat. Add onion and thyme; cook and stir 5 minutes or until onion is tender. Stir in vinegar, salt and pepper, stirring to scrape up browned bits. Transfer onion mixture to medium bowl; stir in cherries.

2 Mash blue cheese and cream cheese in small bowl until blended. Spread evenly over four bread slices. Top each slice with one fourth of cherry mixture (about ⅓ cup) and remaining bread slices.

3 Wipe out skillet. Melt 1 tablespoon butter in same skillet over medium heat. Add two sandwiches; press down with spatula. Cook 3 to 4 minutes per side or until golden brown. Repeat with remaining sandwiches, adding additional 1 tablespoon butter if necessary.

Ham & Cheese Quesadillas with Cherry Jam

Makes 2 servings

1 tablespoon vegetable oil
1 cup thinly sliced red onion
1 small jalapeño pepper, seeded and minced
1 cup pitted fresh sweet cherries
1 tablespoon packed brown sugar

1 teaspoon balsamic vinegar
¼ teaspoon salt
2 (9-inch) flour tortillas
3 ounces ham, thinly sliced
2 ounces Havarti cheese, thinly sliced
2 teaspoons butter

1 For cherry jam, heat oil in large skillet over medium-high heat. Add onion and jalapeño; cook and stir 10 minutes or until onions are golden brown. Add cherries; cook and stir 1 minute. Stir in brown sugar, vinegar and salt. Cook over low heat 1 minute, stirring constantly. Remove from heat; cool slightly.

2 Arrange half of ham slices and half of cheese slices over one side of each tortilla. Top with one fourth of cherry jam. Fold tortillas in half. Reserve remaining jam.

3 Wipe out skillet. Melt butter in same skillet over medium heat. Add quesadillas; press down with spatula. Cook 3 to 4 minutes per side or until golden brown and cheese melts. Cut quesadillas in half; serve with reserved cherry jam.

Hawaiian-Style Burgers

Makes 6 servings

1½ pounds ground beef
⅓ cup chopped green onions
2 tablespoons Worcestershire sauce
⅛ teaspoon black pepper

⅓ cup pineapple preserves
⅓ cup barbecue sauce
6 pineapple slices
6 hamburger buns, split and toasted

1 Combine beef, green onions, Worcestershire sauce and pepper in large bowl. Shape into six (½-inch-thick) patties.

2 Combine preserves and barbecue sauce in small saucepan. Bring to a boil over medium heat, stirring frequently.

3 Spray grid with nonstick cooking spray. Prepare grill for direct cooking over medium heat. Grill patties, covered, 8 to 10 minutes (or uncovered, 13 to 15 minutes) to medium (160°F), turning and brushing often with sauce. Place pineapple on grid; grill 1 minute or until browned, turning once.

4 Serve patties and pineapple on buns.

Broiling Directions Arrange patties on rack in broiler pan. Broil 4 inches from heat until cooked through (160°F), turning and brushing often with sauce. Broil pineapple 1 minute, turning once.

Cookies

Peanutty Double Chip Cookies
Makes about 3 dozen cookies

½ cup (1 stick) butter, softened
¾ cup granulated sugar
¾ cup packed brown sugar
2 eggs
1 teaspoon baking soda
1 teaspoon vanilla

2 cups all-purpose flour
1 cup chunky peanut butter
1 cup semisweet or milk chocolate chips
1 cup peanut butter chips

- -

1 Preheat oven to 350°F. Line cookie sheets with parchment paper or spray with nonstick cooking spray.

2 Beat butter, granulated sugar and brown sugar in large bowl with electric mixer at medium speed until blended. Add eggs, baking soda and vanilla; beat until light and fluffy. Add flour and peanut butter; beat at low speed until dough is stiff and smooth. Stir in chocolate and peanut butter chips.

3 Drop dough by heaping tablespoonfuls 2 inches apart onto prepared cookie sheets. Press down to flatten dough slightly.

4 Bake 12 minutes or until cookies are set but not browned. *Do not overbake.* Remove to wire racks; cool completely.

Crunchy Chocolate Peanut Layer Bars
Makes 2 to 3 dozen bars

1 package (3 ounces) ramen noodles, divided*

1½ cups graham cracker crumbs

½ cup (1 stick) butter, melted

1 can (14 ounces) sweetened condensed milk

1 package (10 ounces) dark chocolate chips

1 cup mini peanut butter cups

1 cup salted roasted peanuts

Use any flavor; discard seasoning packet.

---

1 Preheat oven to 350°F. Spray 13×9-inch baking pan with nonstick cooking spray.

2 Place half of noodles in food processor; process until fine crumbs form. Transfer to large bowl. Add graham cracker crumbs and melted butter; stir until well blended. Press evenly onto bottom of prepared pan.

3 Pour condensed milk over crumb layer; sprinkle with chocolate chips, peanut butter cups and peanuts. Crumble remaining noodles; sprinkle over top.

4 Bake 30 minutes or until set. Cool completely in pan; cut into bars.

Crunchy Bacon & Cheese Cookies

Makes about 4 dozen cookies

¾ cup all-purpose flour

½ teaspoon baking soda

½ teaspoon salt

⅔ cup butter, softened

⅓ cup sugar

1 egg

1 teaspoon vanilla

1¼ cups old-fashioned oats

1 cup (4 ounces) shredded sharp Cheddar cheese

6 slices bacon, crisp-cooked and crumbled

½ cup honey-nut wheat germ*

*Wheat germ is available in most large supermarkets, but a greater variety of brands and flavors is available at most health food stores.

1 Preheat oven to 350°F. Spray cookie sheets with nonstick cooking spray or line with parchment paper. Whisk flour, baking soda and salt in medium bowl.

2 Beat butter and sugar in large bowl with electric mixer on medium speed until light and fluffy. Add egg and vanilla; beat until well blended. Gradually add flour mixture at low speed, beating just until blended. Stir in oats, cheese, bacon and wheat germ.

3 Drop dough by rounded teaspoonfuls 2 inches apart onto prepared cookie sheets.

4 Bake 10 to 12 minutes or until golden brown. Cool on cookie sheets 2 minutes. Remove to wire racks; cool completely.

Caramel Bacon Nut Brownies

Makes 2 to 3 dozen brownies

¾ cup (1½ sticks) butter, cut into pieces

4 ounces unsweetened chocolate, chopped

2 cups sugar

4 eggs

1 cup all-purpose flour

1 package (14 ounces) caramels

¼ cup whipping cream

2 cups coarsely chopped pecans, divided

4 slices bacon, crisp-cooked and crumbled

1 package (12 ounces) chocolate chunks or chips, divided

- -

1 Preheat oven to 350°F. Spray 13×9-inch baking pan with nonstick cooking spray.

2 Combine butter and chocolate in large microwavable bowl; microwave on HIGH 1½ to 2 minutes or until melted and smooth, stirring every 30 seconds. Stir in sugar. Add eggs one at a time, beating until blended after each addition. Stir in flour until blended. Spread half of batter in prepared pan.

3 Bake 20 minutes. Meanwhile, unwrap caramels and place in medium microwavable bowl. Add cream; microwave on HIGH 1½ to 2 minutes or until caramels begin to melt. Stir until smooth. Stir in 1 cup pecans and bacon.

4 Spread caramel mixture over partially baked brownie layer; sprinkle with half of chocolate chunks. Pour remaining brownie batter over top; sprinkle with remaining 1 cup pecans and chocolate chunks. Bake 25 minutes or until set. Cool completely in pan on wire rack. Cut into bars.

Peanut Butter Fudge Whoopies
Makes 14 whoopie pies

1½ cups plus 2 tablespoons all-purpose flour

1 teaspoon baking powder

1 teaspoon baking soda

½ teaspoon salt

1 cup creamy peanut butter, divided

½ cup granulated sugar

½ cup packed brown sugar

¼ cup (½ stick) butter, softened

1 egg

1 teaspoon vanilla

½ cup milk

16 ounces semisweet chocolate, chopped

1½ cups whipping cream

½ cup chopped peanuts (optional)

1 For cookies, whisk flour, baking powder, baking soda and salt in medium bowl.

2 Beat ½ cup peanut butter, granulated sugar, brown sugar and butter in large bowl with electric mixer at medium-high speed until creamy. Add egg and vanilla; beat at medium speed 2 minutes. Add flour mixture and milk; beat at low speed just until combined. Cover and refrigerate 30 minutes.

3 Preheat oven to 350°F. Line two cookie sheets with parchment paper. Drop batter by tablespoonfuls 2 inches apart onto prepared cookie sheets.

4 Bake 14 minutes or until light brown around edges. Cool on cookie sheets 5 minutes. Remove to wire racks; cool completely.

5 For filling, place chocolate and remaining ½ cup peanut butter in large bowl. Bring cream to a simmer in microwave or in small saucepan over low heat. Pour over chocolate and peanut butter. Let stand 2 minutes; stir until well blended. Refrigerate 30 minutes or until firm. Beat with electric mixer at medium-high speed until thick and creamy.

6 Pipe or spread filling on flat side of half of cookies; top with remaining cookies. Place peanuts in shallow dish; roll edges of cookies in peanuts, if desired.

Caramel Chocolate Chunk Blondies
Makes 2 to 3 dozen blondies

1½ cups all-purpose flour
1 teaspoon baking powder
1 teaspoon fine salt
¾ cup granulated sugar
¾ cup packed brown sugar
½ cup (1 stick) butter, softened
2 eggs

1½ teaspoons vanilla
1 package (11½ ounces) semisweet chocolate chunks or 10 ounces chopped bittersweet chocolate
5 tablespoons caramel ice cream topping
Flaky sea salt (optional)

1 Preheat oven to 350°F. Line 13×9-inch baking pan with parchment paper or spray with nonstick cooking spray. Whisk flour, baking powder and 1 teaspoon salt in medium bowl.

2 Beat granulated sugar, brown sugar and butter in large bowl with electric mixer at medium speed until smooth and creamy. Add eggs and vanilla; beat until well blended. Gradually add flour mixture at low speed, beating just until blended. Stir in chocolate chunks.

3 Spread batter evenly in prepared pan. Drop spoonfuls of caramel topping over batter; swirl into batter with knife. Sprinkle with sea salt, if desired.

4 Bake about 30 minutes or until edges are golden brown (center will be puffed and will not look set). Cool completely in pan on wire rack. Remove from pan using parchment; cut into bars.

Salted Caramel Chocolate Thumbprint Cookies

Makes 2½ dozen cookies

1½ cups all-purpose flour
¾ cup unsweetened cocoa powder
½ teaspoon salt
1 cup (2 sticks) butter, softened
⅔ cup packed brown sugar
2 eggs, separated
1 teaspoon vanilla
2 cups finely chopped pecans

Caramel Filling

½ cup packed brown sugar
¼ cup (½ stick) butter
2 tablespoons whipping cream
¼ teaspoon salt
2 tablespoons powdered sugar

1 Preheat oven to 375°F. Line cookie sheets with parchment paper or leave ungreased. Whisk flour, cocoa and ½ teaspoon salt in small bowl.

2 Beat butter and ⅔ cup brown sugar in large bowl with electric mixer at medium speed until light and fluffy. Beat in egg yolks and vanilla until well blended. Gradually add flour mixture at low speed, beating just until blended. Shape level tablespoonfuls of dough into balls.

3 Whisk egg whites in small bowl. Place pecans in medium bowl. Dip balls one at a time into egg whites, turning to coat completely and letting excess drip back into bowl. Roll in pecans to coat. Place on prepared cookie sheets. Press thumb firmly into center of each cookie.

4 Bake about 10 minutes until cookies are set. Quickly repress thumbprints with end of wooden spoon. Cool on cookie sheets 5 minutes. Remove to wire rack; cool completely.

5 For filling, combine ½ cup brown sugar and ¼ cup butter in small saucepan. Cook over medium heat until mixture begins to boil, stirring constantly; boil 1 minute, stirring constantly. Remove from heat. Stir in cream and ¼ teaspoon salt; cool 15 minutes. Whisk in powdered sugar until smooth. Working quickly, fill each cookie with about ½ teaspoon filling; let stand until firm.

White Chocolate Toffee Almond Bars

Makes 2 to 3 dozen bars

2¼ cups all-purpose flour
2 tablespoons instant espresso or instant coffee granules
1 teaspoon fine salt
1 cup (2 sticks) butter, softened
1 cup sugar

1 egg
1 teaspoon almond extract
⅔ cup sliced almonds
⅓ cup toffee bits
⅔ cup white chocolate chips
Flaky sea salt

1 Preheat oven to 350°F. Spray 13×9-inch baking pan with nonstick cooking spray. Whisk flour, espresso and 1 teaspoon salt in medium bowl.

2 Beat butter and sugar in large bowl with electric mixer at medium-high speed until light and fluffy. Add egg and almond extract; beat until blended. Gradually add flour mixture at low speed, beating just until blended. Stir in almonds, toffee bits and white chips. Spread dough evenly in prepared pan. Sprinkle with sea salt.

3 Bake 23 to 28 minutes or until center is set and edges are lightly browned. Cool completely in pan on wire rack. Cut into bars.

Classic Chocolate Chip Cookies
Makes about 2 dozen cookies

1¼ cups all-purpose flour
½ teaspoon fine salt
½ teaspoon baking soda
½ cup (1 stick) butter, softened
½ cup granulated sugar

¼ cup packed brown sugar
1 egg
1 teaspoon vanilla
1 cup semisweet or bittersweet chocolate chips
Coarse salt or flaky sea salt

1 Preheat oven to 350°F. Line cookie sheets with parchment paper. Whisk flour, ½ teaspoon salt and baking soda in medium bowl.

2 Beat butter, granulated sugar and brown sugar in large bowl with electric mixer at medium speed until light and fluffy. Add egg and vanilla; beat until well blended. Add flour mixture; beat at low speed just until blended. Stir in chocolate chips.

3 Drop dough by tablespoonfuls 2 inches apart onto prepared cookie sheets. Sprinkle tops with coarse salt.

4 Bake 10 to 12 minutes or until edges are lightly browned. Cool on cookie sheets 1 minute. Remove to wire racks; cool completely.

Note For best flavor, wrap dough in plastic wrap and refrigerate overnight or up to 2 days.

Desserts

Salted Caramel Quinoa

Makes 6 servings

1 cup uncooked quinoa
2 cups water
1 teaspoon fine salt
2 cups whole milk
½ cup packed dark brown sugar

1 teaspoon vanilla
2 tablespoons caramel ice cream topping
Sliced almonds (optional)
Flaky sea salt

----

1 Place quinoa in fine-mesh strainer; rinse well under cold water.

2 Bring 2 cups water in medium saucepan to a boil over high heat; stir in quinoa and 1 teaspoon salt. Reduce heat to low; cover and simmer 10 to 15 minutes or until quinoa is tender and water is absorbed.

3 Add milk, brown sugar and vanilla. Bring to a boil over medium heat; cook 5 to 10 minutes until thickened, stirring frequently.

4 Scoop pudding into serving bowls. Cool slightly; pudding will thicken upon standing. Drizzle caramel topping over top; sprinkle with almonds, if desired, and flaky salt.

Turtle Cheesecake
Makes 12 servings

Crust

½ cup (1 stick) butter

4 ounces semisweet baking chocolate, chopped

½ cup sugar

2 eggs

½ teaspoon salt

½ teaspoon vanilla

¾ cup all-purpose flour

½ cup finely chopped pecans

Filling

4 packages (8 ounces each) cream cheese, softened

1 cup sugar

1½ teaspoons vanilla

½ cup sour cream

4 eggs

½ cup caramel topping

Toppings

½ cup chopped pecans

2 tablespoons caramel topping

¼ teaspoon salt

1 cup prepared fudge frosting

- -

1 Preheat oven to 350°F. Spray 9-inch springform pan with nonstick cooking spray. Wrap outside of pan with foil.

2 For crust, melt butter and chocolate in medium saucepan over low heat, stirring frequently until smooth. Remove from heat; stir in ½ cup sugar until blended. Add 2 eggs one at a time, stirring until well blended after each addition. Stir in ½ teaspoon salt and ½ teaspoon vanilla. Stir in flour and ½ cup pecans just until blended. Spread evenly in prepared pan. Bake 15 minutes or until top is set but still soft. Remove from oven and place in larger baking pan.

3 For filling, beat cream cheese in large bowl with electric mixer at low speed until creamy. Add 1 cup sugar and 1½ teaspoons vanilla; beat until well blended. Add sour cream; beat until blended. With mixer running at medium speed, add 4 eggs one at a time, beating until well blended after each addition. Spread half of filling over crust. Drop ¼ cup caramel topping by teaspoonfuls over filling; swirl with skewer or knife. Top with remaining filling. Drop remaining ¼ cup caramel topping

by teaspoonfuls over filling; swirl with skewer. Place pan in oven; add hot water to larger pan to come halfway up side of springform pan.

4 Bake 1 hour or until top of cheesecake is almost set. Immediately run knife around side of cheesecake to loosen. Cool completely in pan on wire rack. Refrigerate 4 hours or overnight.

5 For nut topping, cook and stir ½ cup pecans in small skillet over medium-low heat 3 to 5 minutes or until fragrant and lightly browned. Add 2 tablespoons caramel topping and ¼ teaspoon salt; cook 1 minute or until nuts are glazed. Spread over top of cheesecake. Place frosting in piping bag or large resealable food storage bag fitted with large star tip. Pipe rosettes around edge of cheesecake.

Chocolate Chip Doughnuts
Makes 12 doughnuts

1 cup all-purpose flour
½ cup granulated sugar
2 tablespoons cornstarch
2 teaspoons baking powder
½ teaspoon fine salt
1 cup semisweet chocolate chips
½ cup milk

6 tablespoons butter, melted
1 egg
¼ cup (½ stick) butter
1½ cups powdered sugar
1½ tablespoons milk or cream
Coarse or flaky sea salt

----

1   Preheat oven to 425°F. Spray 12 cavities of doughnut pan with nonstick cooking spray.

2   Combine flour, sugar, cornstarch, baking powder and ½ teaspoon salt in medium bowl; mix well. Add chocolate chips; toss to coat with flour. Whisk milk, melted butter and egg in medium bowl until well blended. Stir into flour mixture until smooth and well blended.

3   Spoon batter into large resealable food storage bag. Cut small corner from bag. Pipe mixture evenly into prepared cups, filling half full.

4   Bake 7 to 9 minutes or until doughnuts are puffed and golden. Cool in pan on wire rack 3 to 5 minutes. Remove to wire rack; cool completely.

5   For glaze, cook butter in small saucepan over medium heat until foaming has subsided and butter is golden brown with a nutty smell. Whisk in powdered sugar and 1½ tablespoons milk; cook 1 minute, whisking constantly. Working quickly, dip tops of doughnuts into glaze; place on wire rack and immediately sprinkle with coarse salt. If glaze hardens, rewarm briefly over low heat.

Peanut Butter & Chocolate Swirls

Makes 12 servings

1 package (8 ounces) crescent roll sheet

⅔ cup semisweet chocolate chips

3½ tablespoons whipping cream, divided

⅓ cup plus 2 tablespoons peanut butter, divided

¼ cup packed brown sugar

¼ cup finely chopped roasted peanuts

---

1 Preheat oven to 350°F. Spray 12 standard (2½-inch) muffin cups with nonstick cooking spray.

2 Unroll crescent roll dough on work surface. Combine chocolate chips and 2 tablespoons cream in medium microwavable bowl; microwave on HIGH 30 seconds. Stir until chocolate is melted and mixture is smooth. Place ⅓ cup peanut butter in small microwavable bowl; microwave on HIGH 20 seconds or just until softened. Spread peanut butter over dough to within ½ inch of edges; sprinkle with brown sugar, pressing lightly into peanut butter. Spread two thirds of chocolate mixture over brown sugar; sprinkle with peanuts. Tightly roll up dough; pinch seam to seal. Make sure roll is 12 inches long before cutting crosswise into 1-inch slices. Place slices cut sides up in prepared muffin cups.

3 Bake 12 minutes or until golden brown. Cool in pan 2 minutes; use small spatula or knife to loosen edges. Remove to wire rack set over sheet of waxed paper.

4 Add remaining 1½ tablespoons cream to remaining chocolate mixture; microwave on HIGH 10 to 20 seconds or until mixture is smooth and thinned to glaze consistency. Place remaining 2 tablespoons peanut butter in small microwavable bowl; microwave on HIGH 30 seconds or until melted. Drizzle chocolate mixture and peanut butter over rolls. Serve warm or at room temperature.

Honey-Roasted Peanut Butter Minis

Makes 28 mini cupcakes

1¼ cups all-purpose flour

1 teaspoon baking powder

¼ teaspoon salt

⅔ cup packed brown sugar

½ cup creamy peanut butter

¼ cup vegetable oil

1 egg

2 tablespoons honey

½ cup milk

⅔ cup chopped honey roasted peanuts, divided

Honey Peanut Butter Frosting (recipe follows)

1 Preheat oven to 350°F. Line 28 mini (1¾-inch) muffin cups with paper baking cups. Whisk flour, baking powder and salt in medium bowl.

2 Combine brown sugar, peanut butter, oil, egg and honey in large bowl; stir until well blended and smooth. Add flour mixture and milk; mix just until combined. Stir in ⅓ cup chopped peanuts. Spoon batter evenly into prepared muffin cups.

3 Bake 12 to 15 minutes or until toothpick inserted into centers comes out clean. Cool in pans 5 minutes. Remove to wire racks; cool completely.

4 Prepare Honey Peanut Butter Frosting. Pipe or spread frosting on cupcakes; sprinkle with remaining ⅓ cup chopped peanuts.

Honey Peanut Butter Frosting Combine ⅔ cup creamy peanut butter, ¼ cup (½ stick) softened butter and ¼ cup honey in large bowl; stir until smooth. Stir in 1 cup powdered sugar until well blended.

Chocolate Peanut Butter Pie
Makes 8 servings

10 whole chocolate graham crackers, broken into pieces

2 tablespoons granulated sugar

¼ cup (½ stick) butter, melted

1 package (8 ounces) cream cheese, softened

1 cup creamy peanut butter

1¾ cups powdered sugar, divided

3 tablespoons butter, softened

1¾ teaspoons vanilla, divided

¼ teaspoon salt

2 cups cold whipping cream

½ cup unsweetened cocoa powder

2 packages (1½ ounces each) chocolate peanut butter cups, chopped

----

1 Preheat oven to 350°F. Combine graham crackers and granulated sugar in food processor; process until finely ground. Add ¼ cup melted butter; process until well blended. Press onto bottom and up side of 9-inch pie plate.

2 Bake 8 minutes. Cool completely on wire rack.

3 Meanwhile, beat cream cheese, peanut butter, ¾ cup powdered sugar, 3 tablespoons softened butter, 1 teaspoon vanilla and salt in large bowl with electric mixer at medium speed about 3 minutes or until light and fluffy. Spread filling in cooled crust; smooth top. Refrigerate pie while preparing topping.

4 Whip cream, remaining 1 cup powdered sugar, ¾ teaspoon vanilla and cocoa in medium bowl with electric mixer fitted with whisk attachment at high speed 1 to 2 minutes or until soft peaks form. Spread chocolate whipped cream over peanut butter layer; sprinkle with peanut butter cups. Refrigerate several hours or overnight.

Maple Bacon Cupcakes

Makes 12 cupcakes

Cupcakes

1½ cups all-purpose flour
1¾ teaspoons baking powder
¼ teaspoon salt
¾ cup granulated sugar
½ cup (1 stick) butter, softened
2 eggs
2 tablespoons maple syrup

½ cup milk
8 slices bacon, crisp-cooked and
    finely chopped, divided

Maple Frosting

½ cup (1 stick) butter, softened
3 tablespoons maple syrup
2 tablespoons milk
3 cups powdered sugar

1. Preheat oven to 350°F. Line 12 standard (2½-inch) muffin cups with paper baking cups. Whisk flour, baking powder and salt in medium bowl.

2. Beat granulated sugar and ½ cup butter in large bowl with electric mixer at medium speed until light and fluffy. Add eggs and 2 tablespoons maple syrup; beat until well blended. Add flour mixture and ½ cup milk; beat at low speed just until combined. Reserve 2 tablespoons bacon for topping; stir remaining bacon into batter. Divide batter evenly among prepared muffin cups.

3. Bake 15 to 18 minutes or until toothpick inserted into centers comes out clean. Cool in pan 5 minutes. Remove to wire rack; cool completely.

4. For frosting, beat ½ cup butter, 3 tablespoons maple syrup and 2 tablespoons milk in large bowl with electric mixer at low speed 1 minute. Add powdered sugar; beat at medium speed until fluffy. Frost cupcakes; top with reserved bacon.

Chocolate Peanut Butter Doughnuts
Makes 18 to 20 doughnuts

1½ cups all-purpose flour

2 tablespoons cornstarch

¾ teaspoon baking powder

½ teaspoon salt

¼ teaspoon baking soda

¼ teaspoon ground nutmeg

½ cup granulated sugar

1 egg

¼ cup (½ stick) butter, melted

2 ounces bittersweet chocolate, melted

½ teaspoon vanilla

¼ cup buttermilk

Filling

¼ cup (½ stick) butter, softened

6 tablespoons creamy peanut butter

2 cups powdered sugar

⅛ teaspoon salt*

3 tablespoons whipping cream

¼ cup bittersweet chocolate chips, melted

*Taste before adding salt; some peanut butter may not need additional salt.

----

1 Whisk flour, cornstarch, baking powder, salt, baking soda and nutmeg in large bowl.

2 Beat granulated sugar and egg in large bowl with electric mixer at high speed 3 minutes or until pale and thick. Stir in melted butter, 2 ounces melted chocolate and vanilla. Add flour mixture alternately with buttermilk, mixing at low speed after each addition. Add melted chocolate; mix until well blended. Press plastic wrap directly onto surface of dough. Refrigerate at least 1 hour.

3 Pour about 2 inches of oil into Dutch oven or large heavy saucepan; clip deep-fry or candy thermometer to side of pot. Heat over medium-high heat to 360°F to 370°F.

4 Meanwhile, generously flour work surface. Turn out dough onto work surface. Dust top with flour and roll dough about ¼-inch thick; cut out circles with 2-inch biscuit cutter. Gather and reroll scraps. Line large wire rack with paper towels.

5 Working in batches, add doughnuts to hot oil. Cook 2 minutes, turning twice. Do not crowd pan and adjust heat to maintain temperature during frying. Cool on wire racks.

6 For filling, beat ¼ cup butter and peanut butter in large bowl with electric mixer at medium speed until smooth. Add powdered sugar and salt, if desired; beat at medium speed until well blended. Add cream; beat at high speed 3 minutes or until very light and fluffy. Place filling in pastry bag fitted with large star tip. Cut rounded tops off of doughnuts; pipe about 2 tablespoons filling onto doughnuts and replace tops. Drizzle with melted chocolate.

Chocolate Maple Bacon Bundt Cake

Makes 12 to 16 servings

1 package (about 15 ounces) chocolate cake mix

1 package (4-serving size) chocolate instant pudding mix

4 eggs

¾ cup water

¾ cup sour cream

½ cup bacon fat (see Note)

1 cup semisweet chocolate chips

Maple Glaze

2 tablespoons butter, softened

2 tablespoons maple syrup

1½ cups powdered sugar

2 to 4 tablespoons milk

4 slices bacon, crisp-cooked and crumbled

1 Preheat oven to 350°F. Generously spray 12-cup (10-inch) bundt or tube pan with nonstick cooking spray or baking spray.

2 Beat cake mix, pudding mix, eggs, water, sour cream and bacon fat in large bowl with electric mixer at medium speed 1 to 2 minutes or until well blended. Stir in chocolate chips; pour into prepared pan.

3 Bake 55 to 60 minutes or until cake springs back when lightly touched and toothpick inserted near center comes out clean. Cool in pan on wire rack 1 hour. Invert cake onto serving plate; cool completely.

4 Meanwhile for glaze, whisk butter and maple syrup in medium bowl until blended. Gradually whisk in powdered sugar and 2 tablespoons milk; add additional milk by tablespoonfuls until desired consistency is reached. Pour glaze over cake; sprinkle with crumbled bacon.

Note If you don't have reserved bacon fat on hand, cook 1 pound of bacon in large skillet until crisp; drain bacon on paper towel-lined plate. Drain fat and cool to room temperature. Pour into liquid measuring cup and add melted butter or vegetable oil to measure ½ cup. Set aside four bacon slices for topping; reserve remaining bacon for another use.

Peanut Caramel Cream Pie

Makes 8 to 10 servings

Crust

1½ cups vanilla wafer cookie crumbs

3 tablespoons sugar

2 tablespoons unsweetened cocoa powder

¼ cup (½ stick) butter, melted

Filling

2 cups whipping cream

1 package (8 ounces) cream cheese, softened

¾ cup dulce de leche

¼ cup sugar

1 teaspoon vanilla

2 chocolate-covered peanut-nougat-caramel candy bars (1.86 ounces each), finely chopped

Topping

¼ cup dulce de leche

3 tablespoons milk

½ cup semisweet chocolate chips

1½ teaspoons coconut oil

2 chocolate-covered peanut-nougat-caramel candy bars (1.86 ounces each), coarsely chopped

¼ cup coarsely chopped salted peanuts

----

1   For crust, preheat oven to 350°F. Combine cookie crumbs, 3 tablespoons sugar and cocoa in medium bowl; mix well. Stir in butter until moistened and well blended. Press mixture onto bottom and up side of 9-inch deep-dish pie plate. Bake 8 minutes. Cool completely on wire rack.

2   For filling, whip 2 cups cream in large bowl with electric mixer fitted with whisk attachment at medium-high speed 1 minute or until stiff peaks form. Transfer cream to medium bowl. (Do not wash out mixer bowl.)

3   Combine cream cheese, ¾ cup dulce de leche, ¼ cup sugar and vanilla in same large bowl. Replace whisk with paddle attachment; beat at medium speed 1 to 2 minutes or until well blended, scraping bowl and beater once.

4   Gently fold in whipped cream in three additions until well blended (no streaks of white remain). Fold in two chopped candy bars. Spread evenly in prepared crust. Refrigerate 4 hours or overnight.

5 For topping, microwave ¼ cup dulce de leche in small bowl on HIGH 20 seconds. Stir; microwave 10 seconds or until softened. Stir in milk until well blended. Combine chocolate and coconut oil in small saucepan; heat over low heat until chocolate is melted and mixture is smooth, stirring frequently. Sprinkle 2 chopped candy bars and peanuts over top of pie; drizzle with dulce de leche and chocolate mixtures. Refrigerate until topping is set.

Sweet & Salty Cupcakes
Makes 12 cupcakes

1¼ cups all-purpose flour

1 cup sugar

⅓ cup unsweetened Dutch process cocoa powder

1 teaspoon baking soda

½ teaspoon baking powder

½ teaspoon salt

½ cup buttermilk

½ cup coffee

¼ cup vegetable oil

1 egg

½ teaspoon vanilla

1 cup semisweet chocolate chips

½ cup whipping cream

¾ cup honey roasted peanuts, coarsely chopped

¾ cup coarsely chopped pretzels

¼ to ½ cup caramel sauce

1 Preheat oven to 350°F. Line 12 standard (2½-inch) muffin cups with paper baking cups.

2 Whisk flour, sugar, cocoa, baking soda, baking powder and salt in large bowl. Whisk buttermilk, coffee, oil, egg and vanilla in medium bowl until blended. Add to flour mixture; stir until well blended. Spoon batter evenly into prepared muffin cups.

3 Bake 15 to 18 minutes or until toothpick inserted into centers comes out clean. Cool in pan 5 minutes. Remove to wire rack; cool completely.

4 Place chocolate chips in medium bowl. Bring cream to a simmer in small saucepan over medium heat; pour over chocolate chips. Let stand 5 minutes, then stir until blended and smooth. Set aside about 20 minutes to thicken.

5 Dip tops of cupcake in ganache; return to wire rack. Sprinkle with peanuts and pretzels. Drizzle with caramel topping just before serving.

Tip These cupcakes are best served the day they are assembled. You can bake the cupcakes a day in advance and top with ganache, peanuts, pretzels and caramel sauce the next day. The pretzels and peanuts will become soggy if they are sprinkled on the cupcakes too early.

Salted Caramel Banana Cobbler
Makes 8 to 10 servings

8 medium bananas (firm, yellow, no spots), cut into ½-inch slices (about 6 cups)

¾ cup sugar, divided

¾ teaspoon salt, divided

2 tablespoons water

6 tablespoons butter, divided

⅓ cup plus ¼ cup whipping cream, divided

1 cup all-purpose flour

1½ teaspoons baking powder

½ cup bittersweet chocolate chips

1 egg, lightly beaten

---

1   Preheat oven to 375°F. Spray 8-inch square baking dish with nonstick cooking spray. Place bananas in large bowl.

2   Combine ½ cup sugar, ½ teaspoon salt and water in medium heavy saucepan; bring to a boil over medium-high heat. Cook about 4 minutes or until sugar is deep amber color, swirling pan occasionally. Remove from heat; carefully add 2 tablespoons butter and whisk until melted. Slowly pour in ⅓ cup cream (mixture will spatter). Once spattering has stopped, whisk until mixture is well blended and smooth. Return saucepan to medium-high heat; cook 1 minute or until slightly thickened, stirring constantly. Pour over bananas; stir until evenly coated. Spoon into prepared baking dish.

3   Whisk flour, remaining ¼ cup sugar, ¼ teaspoon salt and baking powder in medium bowl. Cut remaining 4 tablespoons butter into small pieces. Add butter to flour mixture; mix with fingertips until shaggy clumps form. Stir in chocolate chips. Add remaining ¼ cup cream and egg; stir just until combined. Drop topping, 2 tablespoons at a time, into mounds over banana mixture.

4   Bake about 40 minutes or until filling is bubbly and topping is golden brown.

Turtle Dump Cake
Makes 12 to 16 servings

1 package (about 15 ounces) devil's food cake mix

1 package (4-serving size) chocolate instant pudding and pie filling mix

1½ cups milk

1 cup chopped caramels

1 cup semisweet chocolate chips

½ cup pecan pieces

½ teaspoon coarse or flaky sea salt

- -

1 Preheat oven to 350°F. Spray 13×9-inch baking pan with nonstick cooking spray.

2 Combine cake mix, pudding mix and milk in large bowl; beat 1 to 2 minutes or until well blended. Spread batter in prepared pan; top with caramels, chocolate chips and pecans. Sprinkle with salt.

3 Bake 30 to 35 minutes or until toothpick inserted into center comes out clean. Cool in pan at least 15 minutes before serving.

Snacks

Salted Caramel Pops
Makes 12 pops

1 pint (2 cups) vanilla ice cream
1 cup finely chopped salted pretzel sticks (about 2 cups whole pretzels)

¼ cup caramel ice cream topping
Coarse salt
Pop sticks
2 ounces semisweet chocolate

- -

1 Scoop ice cream into chilled large metal bowl. Cut in pretzels and caramel topping with pastry blender or two knives; fold and cut again. Repeat, working quickly, until mixture is evenly incorporated. Cover and freeze 1 hour.

2 Line small baking sheet with plastic wrap. Scoop 12 balls of ice cream mixture onto prepared baking sheet. Freeze 1 hour.

3 Shape ice cream into balls, if necessary. Evenly sprinkle ice cream balls with salt. Insert sticks. Freeze 1 hour or until firm.

4 Melt chocolate in top of double boiler over simmering water, stirring occasionally.

5 Drizzle melted chocolate over pops. Freeze 30 minutes to 1 hour or until firm.

Chocolate-Covered Bacon
Makes 12 slices

12 slices thick-cut bacon
1 cup semisweet chocolate chips
2 tablespoons shortening, divided

1 cup white chocolate chips or
butterscotch chips

----

1 Preheat oven to 400°F. Thread each bacon slice onto 12-inch bamboo skewer. Place on rack in large baking pan. Bake 20 to 25 minutes or until crisp. Cool completely.

2 Combine semisweet chocolate chips and 1 tablespoon shortening in large microwavable bowl. Microwave on HIGH at 30-second intervals until melted and smooth.

3 Combine white chocolate chips and remaining 1 tablespoon shortening in large microwavable bowl. Microwave on HIGH at 30-second intervals until melted and smooth.

4 Place bacon on waxed paper-lined baking sheets. Drizzle chocolates over bacon. Refrigerate until firm. Store leftovers in refrigerator.

Old-Fashioned Caramel & Candied Bacon Apples

Makes 6 apples

4 to 6 slices thick-cut bacon
¼ to ½ cup packed brown sugar
1 package (14 ounces) caramels

2 tablespoons water
6 wooden pop sticks
6 medium Granny Smith apples

----

1 Preheat oven to 400°F. Line large rimmed baking sheet with foil. Coat both sides of each strip of bacon with brown sugar; place on prepared baking sheet. Bake 18 to 20 minutes or until bacon is crisp, turning once halfway through baking.

2 Unwrap caramels and place in medium saucepan; add water. Cook over medium-low heat until melted and hot, stirring frequently.

3 Insert stick into stem end of each apple. Place crumbled bacon in shallow bowl. Dip apple into caramel, tilting saucepan until apple is coated; let excess caramel drip back into saucepan. Remove excess caramel by scraping bottom of apple across rim of saucepan.

4 Immediately roll apple in crumbled bacon. Place, stick side up, on waxed paper-lined baking sheet. Repeat with remaining apples. Rewarm caramel over low heat, if needed. Refrigerate at least 10 minutes or until caramel is firm.

Kitchen Sink Trail Mix

Makes about 4½ cups

¼ **cup slivered almonds**

¼ **cup coarsely chopped pecans**

1 **to 1¼ cups granola cereal**

½ **cup raisins**

½ **cup multicolored candy-coated chocolate pieces**

⅓ **cup shredded sweetened coconut**

¼ **cup roasted pepitas (pumpkin seeds)**

¼ **cup peanut butter chips**

¼ **cup chopped dried apricots***

¼ **cup coarsely chopped dried cranberries***

¼ **cup white chocolate chips**

1 **teaspoon ground cinnamon**

¼ **teaspoon ground cardamom**

*Spray knife with nonstick cooking spray to prevent sticking when chopping.

1 Preheat oven to 350°F. Spread almonds and pecans on large baking sheet. Bake 8 to 10 minutes or until fragrant and lightly toasted, stirring once or twice. Cool completely.

2 Combine toasted nuts, cereal, raisins, chocolate pieces, coconut, pepitas, peanut butter chips, apricots, cranberries, white chips, cinnamon and cardamom in large bowl; mix well. Store in airtight container.

Party Popcorn
Makes 6 quarts

¼ cup vegetable oil
½ cup unpopped popcorn kernels
1 teaspoon fine salt or popcorn salt
4 ounces almond bark,* chopped

Rainbow nonpareils

*Look for almond bark by the chocolate chips in the baking aisle of the grocery store. It is confectionery coating and does not contain any almonds.

----

1 Line two baking sheets with parchment paper.

2 Heat oil in large saucepan over medium-high heat 1 minute. Add popcorn; cover with lid and cook 2 to 3 minutes or until popcorn slows to about 1 second between pops, carefully shaking pan occasionally.

3 Spread popcorn on prepared baking sheets; immediately sprinkle with salt and toss gently to blend.

4 Melt almond bark according to package directions. Drizzle over popcorn; sprinkle with nonpareils. Let stand until set.

Peanut Butter & Jelly Monkey Biscuits
Makes 12 servings

¼ cup creamy peanut butter

2 tablespoons butter

2¼ cups all-purpose flour

¼ cup sugar

1 tablespoon baking powder

½ teaspoon salt

¼ cup (½ stick) cold butter, cut into small pieces

¾ cup buttermilk

6 tablespoons seedless strawberry jam, or favorite flavor

1 Preheat oven to 350°F. Line 9×5-inch loaf pan with foil, leaving 2-inch overhang. Spray foil with nonstick cooking spray.

2 Combine peanut butter and 2 tablespoons butter in small saucepan; cook and stir over low heat until melted. Cool slightly.

3 Whisk flour, sugar, baking powder and salt in medium bowl. Cut in ¼ cup cold butter with pastry blender or fingertips until mixture resembles coarse crumbs. Stir in buttermilk just until moistened.

4 Turn out dough onto lightly floured surface; knead six to eight times. Pat dough into 8×6-inch rectangle; cut into 1-inch squares. Roll one third of squares in peanut butter mixture to coat; place in single layer in prepared pan. Top with 2 tablespoons jam, dropping jam by spoonfuls evenly over squares. Repeat layers twice.

5 Bake 35 to 40 minutes or until jam is melted and bubbly and biscuits are flaky. Cool in pan on wire rack 10 minutes. Remove biscuits from pan using foil. Serve warm.

Dipped, Drizzled & Decorated Pretzels

Makes 2 dozen pretzels

1 cup semisweet or milk chocolate chips

1 cup white chocolate chips

1 cup butterscotch or peanut butter chips

24 pretzel rods

Assorted toppings: rainbow sprinkles, chopped nuts, chopped candies, toasted coconut, cookie crumbs and/or decorating sugars

1 Line baking sheet with waxed paper; place wire rack on top. Place chocolate chips, white chocolate chips and butterscotch chips in separate medium microwavable bowls. Microwave chips, one at a time, on HIGH 1 minute; stir. Microwave at 30-second intervals, stirring after each interval, until melted and smooth.

2 Dip half of each pretzel rod into one flavor of melted chips; sprinkle with, or roll in, toppings. Drizzle some dipped pretzel rods with contrasting flavor of melted chips. (Drizzle melted chocolate from spoon while rotating pretzel, to get even coverage.)

3 Place decorated pretzels on prepared wire rack; let stand until set. Do not refrigerate.

Peanut Butter & Banana S'mores
Makes 4 servings

2 tablespoons creamy peanut butter

4 graham crackers, broken in half

1 medium ripe banana, cut into 12 to 16 slices

4 large marshmallows

2 tablespoons chocolate syrup

1 Spread peanut butter evenly over four cracker halves and top each with three to four banana slices and one marshmallow. Place on microwavable plate; microwave on HIGH 15 to 30 seconds until marshmallow puffs.

2 Spoon chocolate syrup over marshmallows and top with remaining cracker halves. Press down lightly.

Tip Coat spoon with nonstick cooking spray before measuring and drizzling syrup to prevent sticking.

Spicy Nuts & Cranberries

Makes about 4 cups

¼ cup (½ stick) butter

¼ cup maple syrup

2¼ cups pecan halves

1 cup whole almonds

¾ cup dried cranberries

¼ cup granulated brown sugar*

½ teaspoon chipotle chili powder or ground red pepper

1 teaspoon salt

*Granulated brown sugar is brown sugar that has been processed to have a light, dry texture similar to granulated sugar. It can be found in the baking aisles of most supermarkets. Or substitute lightly packed regular brown sugar.

1 Preheat oven to 325°F. Line baking sheet with foil; generously grease foil.

2 Combine butter and maple syrup in large saucepan; cook and stir over low heat until butter is melted. Remove from heat. Add pecans, almonds, cranberries, brown sugar, chili powder and salt to saucepan; stir until nuts and cranberries are well coated. Spread mixture on prepared baking sheet.

3 Bake 20 to 25 minutes or until nuts are aromatic and golden brown, stirring every 10 minutes. Mixture will be saucy; glaze will firm up as it cools. Cool completely on baking sheet, stirring occasionally to separate into individual nuts and small clusters. Store in airtight container.

Trail Mix Truffles
Makes 16 truffles

⅓ cup dried apples

¼ cup dried apricots

¼ cup apple butter

2 tablespoons golden raisins

1 tablespoon creamy peanut butter

Pinch of salt

½ cup granola

4 tablespoons graham cracker crumbs, divided

¼ cup mini chocolate chips

1 tablespoon water

1 Combine apples, apricots, apple butter, raisins, peanut butter and salt in food processor or blender; process until smooth. Stir in granola, 1 tablespoon graham cracker crumbs, chocolate chips and water. Shape mixture into 16 balls.

2 Place remaining 3 tablespoons graham cracker crumbs in shallow dish; roll balls in crumbs to coat. Cover and refrigerate until ready to serve.

Sweet & Spicy Beer Nuts

Makes 3 cups

2 cups pecan halves

2 teaspoons salt

2 teaspoons chili powder

1 tablespoon olive oil

½ teaspoon ground cumin

¼ teaspoon ground red pepper

½ cup sugar

½ cup beer

1. Preheat oven to 350°F. Line baking sheet with foil.

2. Mix pecans, salt, chili powder, oil, cumin and red pepper in small bowl. Spread on prepared baking sheet. Bake 10 minutes or until fragrant, stirring occasionally. Cool on baking sheet on wire rack.

3. Combine sugar and beer in large saucepan. Heat over medium-high heat until mixture registers 250°F on candy thermometer. Remove from heat; carefully stir in nuts and any loose spices. Spread nuts on baking sheet, separating clusters.

4. Cool completely. Break up any large pieces before serving.

Chocolate Peanut Crunch

Makes about ¾ pound

1 cup milk chocolate chips
½ cup semisweet chocolate chips
2 tablespoons corn syrup

1 tablespoon shortening
½ cup salted roasted peanuts
2 teaspoons vanilla

1 Spray 8-inch square baking pan with nonstick cooking spray.

2 Combine chips, corn syrup and shortening in small heavy saucepan. Cook over low heat until melted and smooth, stirring constantly.

3 Stir in peanuts and vanilla. Spread in prepared pan, distributing peanuts evenly. Refrigerate until firm. Break into pieces.

Popcorn Granola
Makes 8 servings

1 cup quick oats
6 cups air-popped popcorn
1 cup golden raisins
½ cup chopped mixed dried fruit
¼ cup sunflower kernels
2 tablespoons butter

2 tablespoons packed brown sugar
1 tablespoon honey
1 teaspoon salt
¼ teaspoon ground cinnamon
¼ teaspoon ground nutmeg

1 Preheat oven to 350°F. Spread oats on ungreased baking sheet; bake 10 to 15 minutes or until lightly toasted, stirring occasionally.

2 Combine oats, popcorn, raisins, dried fruit and sunflower kernels in large bowl. Cook butter, brown sugar, honey, salt, cinnamon and nutmeg in small saucepan over medium heat until butter is melted. Drizzle over popcorn mixture; toss to coat.

Chocolate Peanut Butter Fondue
Makes 8 servings

⅓ cup sugar

⅓ cup unsweetened cocoa powder

⅓ cup milk

3 tablespoons light corn syrup

2 tablespoons peanut butter

½ teaspoon vanilla

Assorted fresh fruit, pretzel rods and/or pound cake cubes

1 Combine sugar, cocoa, milk, corn syrup and peanut butter in medium saucepan. Cook over medium heat until heated through, stirring constantly. Remove from heat; stir in vanilla.

2 Pour into medium bowl. Serve warm or at room temperature with fruit, pretzels and/or cake cubes for dipping.

Sweet & Spicy Snack Mix

Makes 10 servings

1 egg white
¼ cup sugar
1 tablespoon soy sauce
¼ teaspoon ground red pepper
2 cups spoon-size shredded wheat cereal

2 cups wheat cereal squares
2 cups salted mini-pretzel twists
¼ cup dry-roasted salted peanuts

1 Preheat oven to 300°F. Spray large baking pan with nonstick cooking spray.

2 Whisk egg white in large bowl until foamy. Whisk in sugar, soy sauce and red pepper. Add cereals, pretzels and peanuts; mix well. Spread in even layer on prepared pan.

3 Bake 30 minutes until crisp and golden brown, stirring every 10 minutes. Cool completely on baking sheet on wire rack. Store in airtight container.

Warm Peanut-Caramel Dip
Makes 1¾ cups

¼ cup peanut butter
2 tablespoons milk
2 tablespoons caramel ice cream
   topping

Sliced apples and pretzel sticks
   or pretzel rods

----

1 Combine peanut butter, milk and caramel topping in small saucepan. Cook over low heat until melted and smooth, stirring constantly. Pour into serving bowl.

2 Serve with apple slices and pretzels.

No-Bake Noodle Clusters

Makes 2 dozen clusters

2 cups crisp chow mein noodles

⅔ cup semisweet chocolate chips

½ cup peanut butter chips

½ cup cocktail peanuts

⅓ cup raisins

- -

1 Line two large baking sheets with waxed paper or parchment paper.

2 Place noodles, chocolate chips, peanut butter chips, peanuts and raisins in large microwavable bowl. Microwave on HIGH 1 minute; stir. If necessary, microwave 30 seconds more or until chips are melted. Stir until well blended.

3 Drop noodle mixture by teaspoonfuls onto prepared cookie sheets. Refrigerate 1 hour. Store clusters between sheets of waxed paper in airtight storage container in refrigerator.

Index

Index

Metric Conversion Chart

VOLUME MEASUREMENTS (dry)

$\frac{1}{8}$ teaspoon = 0.5 mL
$\frac{1}{4}$ teaspoon = 1 mL
$\frac{1}{2}$ teaspoon = 2 mL
$\frac{3}{4}$ teaspoon = 4 mL
1 teaspoon = 5 mL
1 tablespoon = 15 mL
2 tablespoons = 30 mL
$\frac{1}{4}$ cup = 60 mL
$\frac{1}{3}$ cup = 75 mL
$\frac{1}{2}$ cup = 125 mL
$\frac{2}{3}$ cup = 150 mL
$\frac{3}{4}$ cup = 175 mL
1 cup = 250 mL
2 cups = 1 pint = 500 mL
3 cups = 750 mL
4 cups = 1 quart = 1 L

VOLUME MEASUREMENTS (fluid)

1 fluid ounce (2 tablespoons) = 30 mL
4 fluid ounces ($\frac{1}{2}$ cup) = 125 mL
8 fluid ounces (1 cup) = 250 mL
12 fluid ounces (1$\frac{1}{2}$ cups) = 375 mL
16 fluid ounces (2 cups) = 500 mL

WEIGHTS (mass)

$\frac{1}{2}$ ounce = 15 g
1 ounce = 30 g
3 ounces = 90 g
4 ounces = 120 g
8 ounces = 225 g
10 ounces = 285 g
12 ounces = 360 g
16 ounces = 1 pound = 450 g

DIMENSIONS

$\frac{1}{16}$ inch = 2 mm
$\frac{1}{8}$ inch = 3 mm
$\frac{1}{4}$ inch = 6 mm
$\frac{1}{2}$ inch = 1.5 cm
$\frac{3}{4}$ inch = 2 cm
1 inch = 2.5 cm

OVEN TEMPERATURES

250°F = 120°C
275°F = 140°C
300°F = 150°C
325°F = 160°C
350°F = 180°C
375°F = 190°C
400°F = 200°C
425°F = 220°C
450°F = 230°C

BAKING PAN SIZES

Utensil	Size in Inches/Quarts	Metric Volume	Size in Centimeters
Baking or Cake Pan (square or rectangular)	8×8×2	2 L	20×20×5
	9×9×2	2.5 L	23×23×5
	12×8×2	3 L	30×20×5
	13×9×2	3.5 L	33×23×5
Loaf Pan	8×4×3	1.5 L	20×10×7
	9×5×3	2 L	23×13×7
Round Layer Cake Pan	8×1½	1.2 L	20×4
	9×1½	1.5 L	23×4
Pie Plate	8×1¼	750 mL	20×3
	9×1¼	1 L	23×3
Baking Dish or Casserole	1 quart	1 L	—
	1½ quart	1.5 L	—
	2 quart	2 L	—